Mom, There's a Man in the
Kitchen and He's
Wearing Your Robe

Mom, There's a Man in the Kitchen and He's Wearing Your Robe

The Single Mother's Guide to
Dating Well without Parenting Poorly

ELLIE SLOTT FISHER

Da Capo
LIFE
LONG

A Member of the
Perseus Books Group

Text design by Trish Wilkinson
Set in 11-point Goudy by the Perseus Books Group

Library of Congress Cataloging-in-Publication Data
Fisher, Ellie Slott.
    Mom, there's a man in the kitchen and he's wearing your robe : the single mother's guide to dating well without parenting poorly / Ellie Slott Fisher.
        p.   cm.
    Includes index.
    ISBN 0-7382-0980-5 (pbk. ; alk. paper)
    1. Single mothers—Life skills guides. 2. Dating (Social customs)
3. Parenting. I. Title.
HQ759.915.F57 2005
646.7'7'086947—dc22   2004025376

First Da Capo Press edition 2005

Published by Da Capo Press
A Member of the Perseus Books Group
www.dacapopress.com

Da Capo Press books are available at special discounts for bulk purchases in the U.S. by corporations, institutions, and other organizations. For more information, please contact the Special Markets Department at the Perseus Books Group, 11 Cambridge Center, Cambridge, MA 02142, or call (800) 255-1514 or (617) 252-5298, or e-mail special.markets@perseusbooks.com.

1 2 3 4 5 6 7 8 9—08 07 06 05

For Debra and Noah

Contents

Introduction

L et's be honest. My parents weren't thrilled when I first
brought Charlie home to meet them. His hair was long, his
jeans were torn and faded, and his Marine-issued combat boots
had seen better days. I was nineteen, deeply in love, and very
confident this relationship signaled the end of my dating. But
nearly twenty years and two children later I found myself
suddenly single, the awful consequence of Charlie's untimely
death.

I used to think the biggest challenge that dating presented
was concealing a less than perfect guy from my parents. Now, as
middle age loomed and I prepared to reenter the dating world,
my parents were no longer waiting up for me.

Instead, my children were.

Fourteen months after I was widowed, I went on my first date
with a man I had barely noticed at a bat mitzvah. I had been
seated at the lavish pink-and-purple affair with Charlie's fraternity brother Simmons, his wife, and several strangers. The mas-
sive, round banquet table and unrelenting music had prohibited
any conversation, so I was unaware that one of the men, Marty,
was single until he asked Simmons for my number.

The prospect of dating had crossed my mind with greater frequency, and I thought this was probably a good place to start since Marty was a friend of a friend. Also, this date, I told myself, didn't qualify as "blind" since I could vaguely recall Marty's face through the fluffy ballet-motif centerpiece.

The first lesson I learned: If an unemployed (as it turned out) accountant takes you to dinner, cuts his salmon into neat little squares, devours them in sequence so as not to upset the grid, and speaks about how well his ex-wife has remarried, it's perfectly okay to let him pick up the check and never see him again.

Second lesson: I was not ready to date yet.

Third lesson: A guy who talks about his ex-wife with explicit emotion—whether it be with fondness or hate—isn't ready to date either.

Fourth lesson: Shoes reveal so much more than you'd expect.

Any man, even one who confuses red with pink and polyester with silk, can walk into a men's clothing store and be fitted with a decent suit and dress shirt. The true test comes when he's left on his own to buy shoes.

Take, for instance, cool-looking suede slip-ons. These mean he's fashion-conscious, youthful, and interested in trends. He'll probably treat you to some neat restaurants.

Outdoorsy, well-worn docksides show a less creative side—he's not a risk taker. Expect occasional regional theater and a lot of movies and quick bites to eat.

Spiffy Italian leather loafers indicate success, a willingness to spend money, and a pride in personal appearance. He'll favor the symphony orchestra to prove he's cultured and a hockey game to show he isn't.

Marty was wearing scuffed, pointy dress shoes. Oh, well.

When friends learned that I had gone out on my first date, they insisted I meet two other men who had been kept waiting in the wings. Pleasant, pony-tailed Joseph drove up in a bright green pickup truck, his arms laden with flowers and two small toys. Smart man. My ten-year-old daughter, Debra, and six-year-old son, Noah, responded to him immediately. That is, after they unwrapped the gifts, took note of his pierced diamond earring, and discovered he also owned a motorcycle.

Lesson Five: Expect your kids' priorities to differ from yours. Children crave attention, and the one thing they fear when you begin dating is the loss of it. A man who dotes on them will help satisfy their needs—though not necessarily yours.

Around the same time I went out with Joseph, I received a call from a well-to-do divorced stockbroker, Al. I was unnerved, having been told ahead of time he was extremely good looking, younger than I, and very wealthy. I opened the door to a barrel-chested, gray-haired man who was not particularly handsome and not young, and his presence left me silently questioning the credentials of the person who fixed me up.

Poor Al. He no sooner climbed out of his Mercedes and entered my house than he had to run to the bathroom. "Good-looking, my foot," I said to my baby-sitter, thinking Al was securely ensconced in the powder room. How was I to know he'd taken a wrong turn? We were both embarrassed when he finally emerged, and although we said nothing about my errant comment, an apparent nervous stomach drew him back to the bathroom three more times before we ever left my driveway. I had little doubt this would be another one-time date. It was, and when it ended I recalled Lesson Two. For the next five months, I took a hiatus.

Then suddenly one day in late spring, when I was outside planting my annuals and dragging my heavy terra-cotta pots to the porch, it dawned on me that life was still unfolding and I wanted to share mine again.

Now there was no one in the wings.

I complained to my girlfriend Frani, whose husband had fixed me up with Joseph. Without my knowledge, she began scouring the personals. At the same time, I shed some of my pride and told parents on my son's soccer team, friends through work and in the neighborhood, and even family that I was ready to date.

Among those who rang my doorbell was a widower in his mid-thirties and a divorced forty-year-old artist. The widower, a tall, nice-looking man who worked in a manufacturing plant and had a five-year-old son, plunged head over heels into our relationship and by the third date had asked me to marry him. Not feeling quite as enthused, I chose to end it instead. The artist? Let's just say that when he drove up to my house in his tiny convertible Karmann Ghia with his shirt off, thus exposing his sun-kissed chest not only to my neighbors but also to my kids, I figured he was finished, too.

Hearing of these disappointments, my more experienced friend Sandra encouraged me to accompany her to a singles event at a trendy outdoor bar on Philadelphia's waterfront. Most women were dressed in fashionably revealing short skirts or shorts. I was wearing a lovely silk three-quarter-length dress, perfect for afternoon tea.

I had a lot to learn.

A couple days later, I arrived at Frani's house to find her on the telephone answering a personal ad. Tired of hearing me complain about being single, she had selected an ad that admittedly sounded intriguing—something about his, mine, and ours. She decided to answer it on my behalf. "Okay, Frani." I was outwardly annoyed, but inwardly curious and pleased that she had taken an interest. "Hang up, I'll answer the ad myself."

I did, and I met a divorced father of four who swept me off my feet. Within three months he proposed and I accepted. I was so caught up in the ensuing whirlwind that I became oblivious of my children's feelings. While I thought I was providing them with a replacement for their father, they saw a man as different from their own dad as Ozzie Osbourne is from Ozzie Nelson.

A few years later my divorce attorney, privy to all the messy details, told me she couldn't understand what had ever possessed me to marry him. "It's the way he proposed," I said. "Any woman would have said yes."

It was Halloween night and my forty-first birthday. I answered my door to find him standing there dressed in a tuxedo, his appearance further enhanced by a clump of adorable trick-or-treaters. A long white limousine sat majestically in the driveway, ready to drive us to the city to see a show.

When we left the theater, a horse and carriage were waiting outside. We climbed into the carriage, snuggled under a blanket, and headed toward the posh Four Seasons Hotel. With the cool night air caressing our faces and the city lights providing a dramatic backdrop, he asked me to marry him.

So I'm a sucker for romance.

About two and a half years after the wedding and my brilliant discovery that the magical night had been a fluke, I happily divorced him. And at forty-five, I was back dating.

As a widow dating I had been very trusting, naively assuming that all marriages were like my first one. As a divorced woman, I spotted red flags even before a guy split the check for a cup of coffee. Added to my own fact-finding mission concerning these men were the voices of my children, now older and a lot more opinionated.

For one thing, having had no choice but to tag along with Mom into a stepfamily, they were now delighted when I dated someone without children. It wasn't a reflection on the man's kids, or on my former stepkids for that matter, but on the impact all children—yours and his—have on a relationship.

When I first began dating as a widow, Noah was fairly undis-criminating about the men as long as they offered to play ball or review his baseball cards. Debra was ten and, because of her age and birth order (she acted as my protector), was less trusting.

The après-divorce dating period found my son eleven and siz-ing up every guy I met: "Too ugly." "He's a girl." "Too nerdy." "Nice car." "His kid's weird." "Wow, he can get us Eagles tickets!" Pubescent boys are pretty clear about their priorities. My daugh-ter was nearly sixteen and had started dating. Not wanting Mom to be alone for the rest of her life, she took an active interest in my dates, helping me select clothes to wear and willingly greet-ing the men at the door.

For the next three years, before Noah morphed into a typi-cally blasé teenaged boy, he could be enlisted to peer through the curtain as a blind date walked from his car to my front door.

"Yep, he's driving a BMW, Mom . . . and, wait a second, yep, he's short."

Let me interject something here, an addition to Lesson Four: Shoes *and* a man's car reveal his soul.

During any particular decade, single men favor a specific model of car, one they think will make them appear to be with it, masculine, and youthful. During this period of my dating life, it was the BMW. Well over half the men who pulled up to my door exited from secondhand ones, spanking new convertibles, rusted-out sedans, or late-model beauties.

As for the stature of the man, I am only five feet two-and-a-half inches, so people have been keen to fix me up with short men. And even though the two men I married were tall, I believe that the single most attractive thing about a man is not his height but his level of self-confidence. A short, balding, totally secure guy is about as sexy as they come.

But I digress.

Now, as a divorced woman I began to understand what my friend Sandra was facing. People say "widow" with a certain amount of deference and respect. They say "divorcée" heavily accenting the Frenchness of the word, as though that says it all. But I say, think of all those people who persist in miserable marriages, and consider yourself fortunate.

A wiser person the second time around, I now examined each date closely. I realized that some men were not who they seemed to be, and I became better at recognizing warning signs. This ability came in handy when I met a soon-to-be-divorced doctor.

The doctor told me he owned a beach house along the New Jersey shore and that, ultimately, his wife would keep that as part of a divorce settlement. In the meantime, he saw nothing wrong with his staying there overnight on the first floor while his estranged wife and her new boyfriend slept upstairs. After all, he reasoned, where else could he go?

Lesson Six: Don't date any man who still has one foot in his former relationship, whether out of longing or spite.

There was also Stan, a widower my age with two daughters. My son mercilessly made fun of him for wearing more gold jewelry than Mr. T, choosing ballet over baseball, and relishing gossip as a pastime. I tried to ignore my son's prejudices about this man. That is, until a bird became trapped in my fireplace and I begged Stan to come over and help me get it out. "I don't do birds," he said. "Ever see that Alfred Hitchcock movie?"

"But I need you."

"Sorry, I don't do birds. By the way, did you hear your old seamstress, Gloria, is getting a divorce? I heard her husband was in . . . "

I deserved better than that.

A short time later, I met a very sweet twice-divorced man at a funeral. Dale's diminutive frame, soft-spoken manner, and gentle movements belied the fact that he was an extreme athlete. His

idea of skiing was to be dropped from a helicopter in the treach-
erous, ungroomed back bowls of the Rockies. My idea of skiing
was a quick run down the greens, a long hot toddy at the base,
and a calming, catatonic hour in the Jacuzzi.

I also love the beach. Slathered in suntan lotion sitting on a
sand chair, I can read for hours, soothed by the sound of the
ocean and the orchestrated buzz of the conversations around me.

"You sit on the beach?" Dale asked over lunch. "In a crowd?"

"It's relaxing," I replied. Plus I am an inquisitive journalist at
heart who loves to watch and listen to people.

Dale told me he viewed the beach differently. He preferred to
alight from a boat two miles off the Atlantic Coast and swim
ashore, using the warm, glittery beach merely as a brief pit stop
before heading back out into the water.

It's too bad I dropped out of Girl Scouts.

✳ ✳ ✳

Occasionally, my children have connected with one of my dates
more than I have; other times they have been delighted to hear
that a relationship was ending. Only once did either of them actually insist I not date a guy. He was Noah's dermatologist, and
at the time I took my son to him for a wart removal, he was a
married man. While freezing Noah's warts, he pummeled me
with questions. "I hear you're dating George, and how is that going? Think you'll get married again? You're getting older, so you
better hurry."

Whoa. My being single didn't entitle this guy to ask me personal questions, especially while he was inflicting pain on my
son. Noah and I left the examination room, knowing our next
appointment would be with his partner. Months later the phone
rang. It was him.

"I don't usually ask out women I meet through my practice, but I'm attracted to you."

"Wait. Aren't you married?"

"What?! Have you been living under a rock? I've been separated for months!" And can you imagine why?

I told him I was involved with someone seriously. I wasn't, but I've never been very good at saying no. I then told Noah about the phone call.

"Mom, there is no way you are going to date that guy!"

I didn't need convincing.

In another instance, I disappointed a fifteen-year-old Noah when I stopped seeing a man with whom he enjoyed talking sports and whose young sons idolized him. This enforced for me the challenges of dating as a mom. It wasn't just my feelings that I needed to consider. It was my kids'.

Twelve years ago, when Charlie and I were watching a television news magazine segment on dating, I derided the singles scene like someone who assumed being married for life was as definite as death and taxes. And now as an unmarried woman, a single mom, half of an uncoupled couple, I was relying on my instincts and experiences to get by in a social world I never dreamed I'd enter.

The experience has been filled with some surprises, the genial widower who held onto my name and number for two years before phoning; much laughter, especially Sunday mornings when my curious girlfriends call for the latest installment; a little disappointment, like the promising prospects that turn out to be flops; and, indeed, lots of fun.

✳ ✳ ✳

This book has evolved from years of my being pulled aside at cocktail parties and invited to lunch by women who are anticipating entering the dating world and have no idea where to begin. How do you meet guys? What do your kids think? How do you get along with his kids? How do you handle the sex? These are questions I am asked over and over again by mothers who last had a date when "hooking up" meant joining together, as in a business merger or a horse and wagon, not having a one-night stand.

According to the U.S. Census Bureau, there are more than ten million single mothers whose children, under the age of eighteen, still live at home. Another twenty-two million children over eighteen live in a home maintained by a single parent. In other words, you are not alone.

I have found that once women, newly widowed or divorced, or soon-to-be divorced, admit to themselves that they want to date, they are impatient to begin. But before they take that first daunting step, they want some advice from women who've been there.

You are about to meet single mothers who, like you, are dating for the first time in years. Join them as they confess to you their triumphs and mistakes. They'll reduce your apprehension about reentering the dating world and guide you in maintaining healthy relationships with your children. Many of these moms have remarried, and others continue to date, some as many as four men a week.

There are worthy, caring available men out there. You just have to learn where to look and how and how not to involve your children. Dating as a mother is tricky. You need to know when it is appropriate to allow your ten-year-old to weigh in on your dating and when it is no one's business but your own. You need to sense when it is right to introduce a date to your kids. You need to feel comfortable having sex but know how to rein in the unexpected, unbridled passion. And you need to be able to talk to your dating teenagers without looking like a hypocrite.

My research for this book has introduced me to remarkable single moms, in their thirties, forties, and fifties, all juggling children, work, and dating. There is Gladys, who had no idea how to be sexual after a twenty-five-year passionless marriage, and Melanie, whose physical transformation gave her the courage to leave her control-freak husband.

You'll cringe when you hear about Rachel getting caught by her teenaged son while in a compromising position, and feel Julie's pain as she finally tells her kids she is in love with a man they have never met.

You'll laugh with Judith as she juggles several men—from the West Coast to the East Coast—and with Cass, who swears off men only to inadvertently slip into the relationship of a lifetime.

You will hear from family therapists who offer excellent advice to dating moms. For example, sex on the kitchen counter when your kids are upstairs sleeping is probably not a sterling idea.

You will become acquainted with some wonderful single fathers, sensitive to the needs of their children as well as to the children of their dates, and to some impressive kids, who, I must admit, I interviewed with trepidation, wary of what I'd learn about my own children's feelings.

This book first prepares you and your children for the prospect of dating. It then covers the developing relationship and discusses how everything you do, from primping for the date to having sex to planning a future with a new man, affects your children. It also deals with your children's relationship with the men you date and includes feedback from both men and children.

So after twelve years off and on as a single mom and twenty-five years as a writer, I have questioned, listened to, and reflected on the comments of people affected in one capacity or another by parental dating. To those single moms out there: Date when you're ready and not when others think you should be. Be honest with your children. They don't need to know you bought the midnight black water-filled bra at Victoria's Secret, but they do need to know you're dating.

Above all, get out there and enjoy yourself.

CHAPTER ONE

Suddenly Uncoupled

Growing up in a traditional family of four with a self-employed dad and a stay-at-home mom, I didn't know any widows, divorcées, stepmoms, or single mothers. Then, within one six-year period of my life, I became all of those.

The hardest description to acclimate to was "single." I loved being married. I loved confiding in my husband about things, particularly our kids, that I discussed with no one else. I loved making plans to get together with other couples over the weekend. I loved being able to say, "My husband is just parking the car."

Here I was *single*, a characterization that took years to slide easily off my tongue. I drove alone to Saturday-night parties, walking several blocks in my heels. I became infuriated when a roofer, knowing he had no husband to contend with, tried to rip me off. I felt resigned every time the well-meaning guy in the hardware store said, "Just get your husband to replace this."

But that was in the beginning.

By virtue of being single, I developed the confidence to attempt things that I never would have handled before. I learned how to repair a running toilet. I became adept at driving any distance and in any city—including auto-clogged Los Angeles. I completed my taxes by myself and on time. And I sued the roofer and won. The only challenge that continued to elude me was getting everyone to stop meddling in my social life.

As a newly single woman, you are dealing with becoming suddenly uncoupled, and to complicate matters, your life has been opened to public scrutiny. What has happened to your privacy? Without warning, it dissolved when the marriage ended. Now even your letter carrier knows about your husband's indiscretions or your emerging need to find your inner self. You lack the protection that usually comes with having a husband.

You feel alone. You feel vulnerable. You feel sorry for yourself. Enough already.

As an unmarried mom you are someone to be reckoned with. You are someone married folks secretly envy because you are succeeding at being a single parent, a circumstance that could just as easily creep into their lives.

And they know that.

"I anger a lot of people because I am doing well," says Carol, a divorced mom of one teenaged boy.

Home improvement stores like Home Depot and Lowe's offer workshops on how to make home repairs. Take one. It will be empowering.

So if being a single mom is so great, why would you ever consider dating again?

It's that joining together of woman and mother. There's no getting away from it. Part of being a woman is how you feel being with a man. When you first think of dating you are often conflicted. Should your maternal instincts smother any desire to be a sexual object? No. Are you a bad mom to leave your kids with a baby-sitter so you can go on a date? Positively not. Can you really, at your age, go through this again? Yes. Do you even want to? Only you can answer that.

But don't base this last decision on whether you feel more secure hanging out with your kids than with a date. You will always choose the kids. When my children's father died, I loved devoting my weekends to watching their hockey games and inviting their friends over for sleepovers. I didn't need a social life. I had my children. As they got older, I began to realize that as much as I loved them, if all of us were to be healthy, happy, and fulfilled, our social lives had to be separate.

Ready, Set, Go

My decision to begin dating resulted from my trusting my own instincts. So I was shocked to realize, just a few months after Charlie's death, that other people thought they knew what was best for me.

One frigid January night I navigated my station wagon toward the home of a boy in my daughter's fourth-grade class. I was apprehensive about spending time with this flawless family of four, but I would do anything to get out of making dinner.

After a meal that one-upped Emeril Lagasse, the table was cleared and the wife led the children to the basement to watch a movie. The husband and I retired to the living room.

"Have you started dating yet?" asked this mid-thirtyish, good-looking, financially well-off man whom I barely knew.

"It's only been four months since my husband died," I sputtered.

"So? So what are you waiting for?" he challenged. "You wait too long and someone will figure something's wrong with you."

I left that night acutely aware that people, and not just my mother, were contemplating my dating life. It was only the beginning. Three years later, when I was engaged to my second husband, a parent on my son's soccer team expressed her surprise that I could remarry so soon.

Opinions about how much time should pass between *your* becoming single and *your* beginning dating are as profuse as bees at a barbeque and about as welcome.

If only these commentators would think with their feet and try to squeeze into your shoes. Instead, they accuse you of waiting too long or not waiting long enough. This personal aspect of your life, in the minds of family, friends, and nosey acquaintances, is fair game.

It took time for fifty-year-old Carol to rebuild her life and strengthen her badly bruised self-esteem following a five-year marriage to a man who cheated on her. Her desire to date was immediate: "It probably took me five minutes to begin dating. I was right out there falling in love right and left."

Divorced women like Carol are more likely to date immediately, while widows think a "respectable" amount of time must pass. In point of fact, there are no rules. As an unmarried woman you are entitled to date whenever you are ready.

Take the case of thirty-eight-year-old Linda, a teacher and a mother of three young daughters. While she was mourning the drug-overdose death of her forty-year-old husband, an unmarried college sweetheart came to pay his respects. Within a month the old flame was rekindled and the two went public with their renewed romance. The neighborhood exploded in a no-holds-barred gossip fest aimed at illuminating Linda's transgressions. Only the single moms gave her a "Way to go, girl!"

Linda's sort of behavior appalls married people, who, according to psychologist and single mom, Barbara Noble, "just don't get it. Sometimes you think it's a lack of empathy. Sometimes you think it's stupidity." Single moms, on the other hand, recognize that Linda, like every other loving mother, married or otherwise, deserves happiness.

As a single woman, your decision to begin dating is strictly personal. No one can make it for you. You'll know when you desire to be held again, to have sex, to have a man to flirt with and to confide in. As a single mom you are already relying heavily on your instincts, so use them when you begin dating. You may not be ready to be embraced by another man just yet. Or you may be fed up with watching other couples dance while you sit alone at a banquet table.

Remember, there is no right or wrong here. If you think you might be ready, give it a try. Go with a friend to a party or peruse the Internet dating sites. See how you feel. Just hanging around single men will give you a sense of whether you're ready to make a steady diet of it. If not, try again later.

Sometimes the realization that you are ready to date comes in the most unexpected way.

Like many widows, forty-year-old Maribeth fantasized about having sex with acquaintances, guys at work, and the carpenter finishing her basement. It kept her going while she was knee-deep in laundry or helping her eleven-year-old daughter and eight-year-old son with their homework. In reality, she couldn't imagine ever sleeping with another man. It had been twenty years, two decades of added poundage and cellulite, which her husband, Anthony, either didn't seem to notice or was too familiar with her insecurity and its damaging effect to ever go there.

Holidays don't have to be lonely. Be proactive and schedule a trip or host a party.

But alone in bed, with her kids asleep down the hall, Maribeth dreamed. She especially dreamed about Tim, a young stockbroker who worked in Anthony's office, seven years younger than Maribeth and seriously involved with another woman. Three months into singlehood, Maribeth got the strangest phone call from Tim.

"I guess I'll marry her," he confided. "There's probably no one better out there."

"Tim, you don't know that," Maribeth counseled. "You can't marry her unless you are 100 percent certain you are in love with her."

"I don't know." He actually whined. "Did you know with Anthony?"

"Without a doubt."

Then he offered, "Maybe we could get together and talk."

Suddenly Maribeth's fantasy and reality seemed not so far apart, and this shift excited her. She decided to meet Tim at his office—Anthony's old office.

That morning, as the doors shut on the school bus and Maribeth lost sight of whether the ornery driver had pulled away before her children were seated, she hopped into the shower. She scrubbed, perfumed, and hot-oiled her hair. The urge to be feminine and sweet-smelling overwhelmed her morning preparations. It's a reflex suddenly single women have.

By the time she entered Anthony's office lobby, Maribeth felt warm and tingly. As she waited for the elevator doors to open, another of her late husband's former colleagues appeared.

"How great to see you, Maribeth." Hugh gave her a small, polite kiss on the cheek as he took her arm and led her into the elevator. "To what do we owe this wonderful visit?"

She had forgotten how overbearing stockbrokers could be.

"I'm meeting Tim Kelley for lunch," Maribeth reluctantly volunteered.

"What a great idea. Mind if I join you two?"

"That would be great." Forcing a smile, Maribeth reminded herself that her fantasy could never infringe on real life anyway. At least not yet.

The three of them sat in a small café, Tim to her left and Hugh across from the two of them. A radiating electricity rendered her slightly drunk. What was she doing? She had been widowed for a few months by a man she desperately loved, and here she was imagining a romance with a guy young enough to be coming to her for dating advice.

This irony was not lost on Maribeth, who had last had a date when Gerald Ford was president.

As the lunch ended, the sexual tension between Maribeth and Tim evaporated. She headed home to meet her kids' bus and felt a little unsettled, not because she knew nothing further would develop between her and Tim, but because she now realized that, despite loving Anthony, she'd like to be with another man.

You will discover what the right timing is for you; let yourself be comfortable with that. Don't gauge your feelings on the magical one-year period well-meaning people seem to think is precisely the length of time needed to recover from divorce or death. That "one year" could be a month for one person and a lifetime for someone else. More important, a woman must feel good in her own skin before entering a new relationship. She needs to deal with any issues that occurred in her last marriage "or she will make the same mistakes and pick the same people," warns Noble.

And trust your instincts. You might go on a couple of dates and then discover that you aren't ready. Two months after I first began dating, I abruptly stopped. Between caring for my young children and adjusting to running a household alone, I had little energy left for a social life. But then Christmas came, and with dreamy visions of trimming the tree, the Nutcracker Suite playing, and cookies baking, I invited over one of the men I had dated. Joseph was already seeing someone else. "I hadn't heard from you for months," he said. "Why now?"

Like I knew. Why was I suddenly craving male companionship? My life was filled with hockey and soccer games, birthday parties, and family excursions to G-rated movies. I had become adept at putting French braids into little girls' hair, tying little boys' skates, and joining my fair share of parent association committees.

I hung up the phone and pondered Joseph's question. Why now? Why had I given up dating only to passionately want to resume again? Because now I wanted to date, not because someone had a man to fix me up with or because my friends told me I should, but because I knew I felt ready. I wanted to spend the holidays not just with my kids, but also with a man.

Joseph's rejection, though disappointing at the time, helped me eliminate any doubt about whether I was ready to date.

It took Sandra a while to get to this point. She had been so elated to end a twenty-year marriage to a philandering husband that dating was the furthest thing from her mind. Four months later, she visited a friend who, after chastising her for not dating, fixed her up with "Slugger." Okay, so Slugger was not worth a lifetime investment, but for Sandra he served as an experience-worthy first date.

"Then my cousin fixed me up," recalls Sandra, whose children were twelve and fourteen at the time. "It was very intense for three weeks, and then he went back to his old girlfriend. It was bizarre. But it made me realize what I was missing."

As with Carol and Sandra, you'll find that as soon as an interest in dating peaks, you will be impatient to begin. You'll expect family and friends to fix you up—some will, most won't—or you'll create your own pool through dating services, the Internet, singles functions, or the guys at work.

What Will the Kids Think?

While you may have been contemplating dating for quite some time, it is doubtful your children have given it a moment's thought. They need time to process this new development.

Psychologist Marion Lindblad-Goldberg explains that with the absence of a live-in dad, you and your children have already undergone a family reorganization. Roles have been reassigned and your children have been given more responsibility. A feeling of security and closeness develops in this newly organized family. Your entering a serious relationship will wreak havoc on the family dynamics.

But don't let that stop you.

A social life is critical not only for you but for your children. And by the time they are grown and out of the house, most children looking back on Mom's dating appreciate its importance. Lindblad-Goldberg says, "They need to see the parent enjoying a social life in order for them to."

Don't serve as a crutch for your child by always being available. Even if you have no plans for yourself, encourage your

> *If your child is invited to a sleepover party, invite some of the other parents over for cocktails or dessert.*

child to get together with friends, to play outside with the neighborhood kids, or to invite kids over to your house. This is why you need your own social life. Children who see Mom being active will feel guilt-free making plans with other kids. Children who forgo hanging out with other kids will spend endless time worrying about Mom.

Finally broaching the subject of dating with your children can be as unnerving as having told your father your senior prom date was twenty-two and drove a convertible. It's compounded by the sense of guilt that is synonymous with single motherhood. How can you consider your own happiness? Believe me, I know it's hard to put your social well-being toward the top of your priority list. But you can and you must. Don't allow your children to guide you in how, when, and whom you should date. The outcome of relying on them as a compass? You'll get lost.

Lindblad-Goldberg suggests breaking the news to your kids by explaining that as much as Mom loves being with her family and her girlfriends, sometimes she wishes to spend time with a man. Discuss with them what they would like to do when you go out.

Would they like a baby-sitter or to go to a friend's house? Would they like something special to eat or to rent a movie? Let them know where you will be and that you will have a cell phone in case of emergency.

If your kids are teenagers, they are experiencing their own "questions about socialization and sexuality," Lindblad-Goldberg says and will *ultimately* understand your desire to spend time with a man.

If you are patient and honest with your children, they will realize that life goes on for Mom much as it does for them.

Despite understanding all of this, Sally, in her early forties, could not find the courage to tell her twelve-year-old daughter about her dating. She scheduled dates when her ex-husband had custody or lied that she was going out with a girlfriend.

Sally acknowledges, "I know I have to tell her but I'm so afraid to. It's ridiculous. She knows her father dates. In fact, she's even been with him when he's had a date. I just know she'll be angry at me."

Mothers like Sally fear their children won't accept their dating so they often decide to relinquish any social forays. But you have to go on with your life. Otherwise you're going to resent your daughter or son for holding you back.

Sexy Mama!

Once you inform your children of your intention to date, you have to become comfortable seeing yourself as a sexual entity. The maternal mind finds a nurturing mother and a sexy woman to be mutually exclusive. Can you picture Betty Crocker having sex? Yet every single mom recognizes she needs to make herself physically attractive if she is going to date.

"I had a nose job," Carol laughs. "I hated myself when I was divorced. I had to do something to make myself more acceptable."

"I went to town," adds Roseanne, a mother of two who fell in love with the first guy she went out with after her divorce. "I had my hair highlighted. I bought tons of matching underwear. I got my nails done. You get way too comfortable when you're married."

"My bills from Victoria's Secret were unbelievable," Sally remarks. "I dressed differently. Tighter clothes, sexier. I wore makeup all the time."

Melanie, a waitress and a mother of two teenagers, a boy and a girl, gained thirty pounds during her marriage to a narcissistic husband. When that marriage finally flickered to an end, Melanie went on

> *"I dress more youthfully now. All of a sudden you are very aware."—Judith*

a diet, losing thirty-seven pounds. She slid into sexier clothing, began a regimen of sit-ups and walking, and let her chin-length hair grow. What was the biggest change noticed by friends and coworkers? Her smile.

Take a look at yourself. If you feel good physically, you will feel better about dating. Consider getting a new haircut or covering the gray. Bleach your teeth. Dress more youthfully without going the exposed-midriff route. If you don't want to join a gym, then begin a regiment of walking—or at least park far away from your supermarket. Eat more fruit and fewer of the snacks you give the kids. And don't eat the leftovers on their plates as you carry them to the sink (we've all been there). This is about feeling good about yourself.

Your kids will notice these changes and they will be proud of you. Even if they don't comment on the difference and even if they can't quite put their finger on what exactly *is* different, they will be able to tell that Mom looks and feels better. Remember, their seeing you as strong and happy takes a burden off them as well.

You will also *feel* sexy. Despite your initial apprehension about sleeping with a new man for the first time in years, you will be amazed how natural it will feel. Become sensual but don't involve the kids in that aspect of your dating. Your fourteen-year-old daughter ought not to accompany you to buy sexy negligees. Your children also don't need to see you in revealing clothes. Recognizing Mom as a sexual object is something most children would rather avoid.

What Lies Ahead

So you've told the kids, made yourself attractive, and readied yourself for that first date. Is it necessary for your children to meet him now? Not if they don't want to. There will be time later if you find yourself dating one man several times or if your relationship becomes serious.

When Maribeth finally decided to go on her first date, her son was nine and her daughter twelve. She told her children that she had met someone at a wedding and he had invited her out to dinner. Her son was matter-of-fact about the news, having been more interested in building a new Lego fire truck with the babysitter. Her daughter was not at all pleased, believing no man could ever replace her father.

The night of the date arrived, and Maribeth's two girlfriends came over to help her pick out an outfit and do her hair. Her son contently lodged himself in the basement. Her daughter stayed overnight at a friend's house. There is no point in subjecting a child to a man who might not make it past the first date.

While you're eagerly planning for a date, it's easy to lose yourself in conversation with your girlfriends about your expectations of the evening. Your children don't need to be privy to this chatter. Whether it's hearing your end of a phone conversation or overhearing you and your friends talking, kids do not want to be unwitting bystanders. They don't want to visualize Mom on a date. Be selective in how much you tell them, and be aware if they are nearby when you're discussing a guy with friends.

Not surprisingly, a child's age often correlates with his or her reaction to Mom's date. At nine, Maribeth's son didn't have the maturity to understand what the date was about and what it could mean for his future. Her daughter, at twelve, understood many of the repercussions of Mom's date yet didn't have the confidence to know how to handle it.

Six years have passed since Maribeth's first date. Her daughter is a freshman in college and her son a sophomore in high school. Now when she dates, her daughter ecstatically asks what her mother will wear and where she is going. Her son, having grown accustomed to having Mom to himself, is not as thrilled.

> Expect your children's views of your dating to change as they get older and begin dating themselves.

Sandra's experience has been different from Maribeth's. She believes her children have always been "okay" about her dating. "I caught my ex-husband in another woman's house," she says. "The kids were six and four when I had to go to this woman's home. They were in the backseat because I couldn't leave them at home. We never really discussed it, but when their dad and I separated eight years later, my daughter said, 'It's because Daddy had an affair, isn't it?' She kept that inside for eight years. She never talked about it. She seemed happy that I was having a social life and still blamed her father."

At a young age, Sandra's daughter had recognized the importance of her mother's happiness. Lindblad-Goldberg tells her single moms that not only are they entitled to have a life, but their appearing content will produce happy children. If you sacrifice, she believes, your children will think they need to do the same when they become adults. Your wish as a mother is to see your children engaged in successful relationships. You are their role model.

Remember, you do not need permission to have your own self-interest at heart. You need to feel good about yourself. You need to feel worthy as a mother and as a woman, and that includes having sexual and romantic relationships.

My dear friend Cass, thrust into single motherhood eight years ago following her divorce from a race car driver, swore off men entirely and refused her friends' offers to fix her up. A year ago her best friend died of cancer and Cass spoke occasionally to the widowed husband and his children. The phone calls turned into frequent e-mails, which evolved into meeting for coffee. Six months after her friend's death, Cass realized that she and her friend's husband were falling in love.

The reaction: How could Cass date her best friend's husband so soon after she had died? How could the husband date Cass so soon after becoming widowed?

The response: They both discovered happiness.

The result: I plan to wear my powder blue sleeveless sheath dress to their wedding.

CHAPTER TWO

Mom Goes Hunting

S andra logged onto her computer, typed in Match.com, and pulled out her palm pilot, keeper of all the passwords that log her onto to the half dozen or so dating sites to which she belongs. She plugged in her requirements: geography, within a twenty-five-mile radius from her Delaware home; age range, forty-two to fifty-five; and religion, Jewish—and one thousand matches turned up.

That's a lot of first dates.

Then, like a violinist fine-tuning her instrument, Sandra sent her fingers flying across the keyboard as she streamlined her search, specifying income, over $100,000; height, over five feet eight inches; and education, a college degree.

This time only two matches appeared.

Welcome to dating in the twenty-first century. Unless you've been squirreled away in a monastery since the first time you were single, you are aware of the changes in dating—most significantly the explosion of Internet personals. While some of the old methods still exist, like matchmaking, some more creative approaches have appeared, including a concept tailored to our hurried lifestyle called *speed dating*.

Dating is now a multi-million-dollar industry that caters to a booming number of single men and women. In the over-forty-five age bracket alone, there are 36.2 million Americans who are single, according to the U.S. Census Bureau. The dating pool is huge, and all you need to do is jump in.

Trust me, it will get easier after you take that first plunge. Start with small steps, like attending one singles event in your neighborhood or scanning your local newspaper's personals. Recognize that everyone, including the men, is in the same boat. And you do not need to explain yourself. It's not only more common today than thirty years ago to find single moms dating but downright expected.

In the process of looking for dates, you will also have to determine how much you should tell your children. You may be reluctant to be truthful about meeting a stranger online, for example. But in reality, this is often the way single people, whether they are in their twenties or forties, meet, and so long as you explain the precautions you'll take—not giving out your home address or phone number and getting together at a public place—your kids will understand. You'll be surprised. Your kids are so computer-minded, they'll probably have fewer qualms about your finding a guy online than you do.

But how much should you involve them in the process? Should you let them peer over your shoulder while you search the Internet? Or read the items you circle in the newspaper personals? Or be privy to the data a dating service gives you? It's better not to. This is about a potential relationship between two adults, and it should be handled with decorum and privacy. Since a person's profile, such as one found through a dating service or online, reveals a lot of personal details, your kids would be exposed to more information about a prospective date of yours than they are entitled to.

If you meet a date at a party or as a fix-up, you will find it easier describing the circumstances to your kids. The man will seem more like a friend once or twice removed than a complete stranger. The guy you met at Jane's party was a friend of her brother, or the man who just called you got your number from your sister. It goes down a little easier.

Even before you get started on the hunt, you must take three critical steps: first, and most important, like who you are; second, you're not perfect, so stop expecting him to be; and third, do not become all-consumed with finding a man. Live a full life regardless of whether stud.com answers your call. You always appear the most attractive to others when you are contently pursuing your own goals.

So while you're checking into organized dating venues, keep an open mind and an active life, and you'll be surprised: Single men are everywhere.

> The produce aisle has spawned a lot of dates: "Do you know how to cook this vegetable?" or "Do you have any idea which one of these types of apples is good for baking?"

Listen to Judith, a divorced mom of two: "I've been introduced by friends and met guys in dance classes. I meet them all the time. The guy in the fish tank place is always overly attentive." Or to Melanie: "You can meet guys at the grocery store or at a wedding."

Do-It-Yourself Prowling

Through various aspects of your life you already have occasions to meet men. Look at some of these opportunities with a fresh perspective—as a dating single mom.

Enjoy your own interests.   You love to dance, discuss books, or practice yoga. So set yourself up in groups that focus on these interests. If you go online or look in your local newspaper, you will find events attended by like-minded people. In these instances, if you meet a single man, you will know immediately you share a similar love. At the very least you will connect with people with whom you have something in common. And they may have a single brother. I enjoy birding, a sport the uninitiated assume is filled with frumpy elderly folks, their socks pulled up, heads tilted skyward. Well, sure. But it also attracts youthful, outdoorsy, intelligent, well-traveled, athletic men. Exactly my type.

Attend your kids' activities. You're already doing this. Spending weekends at your daughter's soccer games or attending the school Christmas pageant is a great way to get to know the other parents in her class. Don't worry about propriety here. Remember, you're single. You're entitled. And you probably already have so much in common with the guy—same neighborhood, same age child, possibly mutual acquaintances. I sat next to a man at a fundraising dinner at my children's school and we bonded immediately when halfway through the night we realized we were both single parents. We dated for over a year.

Join a gym. Come on, we all need it anyway. This has the added benefit of being good for you, which results in your feeling good about yourself. Gyms teem with available single men who are just as anxious as you are to look and feel better about themselves. Just think of all the easy ways to start a conversation: "Excuse me, would you mind spotting me on the bench? Wow, you're lifting *how* many pounds? I can't get this seat lowered on the bike." The most intimidating part of a gym is not the exercising but feeling comfortable in gym clothes. Admittedly, if you look good in a tank top and shorts, go for it. Let your neighbors prattle. If the only gym near you is a slick upscale one and you find that

unappealing, then check out your local Y. They usually have excellent gym facilities at reasonable prices.

Get some culture.   Most cities, and many smaller towns, have
wonderful art museums, theater groups, and orchestras. Frequently, they arrange evenings just for singles. These are nonintimidating venues for meeting guys because, ostensibly, you
are all there for the culture. Check into membership at these facilities so you can participate in their special classes, trips, or
events. And don't be concerned if you can't tell a Van Gogh
from a Van Eyck. Really, who can? This is a great opportunity to
do something to expand your mind regardless of how many guys
you meet.

Go back to school.   Take a course, any sort that you would enjoy,
such as cooking or college-level, or continuing-education classes.
Maybe you've always wanted to study French or astrology. It's not
only another way to meet men with interests similar to yours, but
you're expanding your knowledge in the process. And that makes
you far more interesting to be around. These courses are available
throughout the year at local colleges and high schools. You never
know where things will lead. I met a guy in my graduate program
who, although married, had a single brother I dated. Also, my
married girlfriend Susie fixed me up with her art teacher. Come
to think of it, why not convince your married friends to go back
to school, too?

Spend weekends at Starbucks.   I'm not kidding. This place is over-
run with guys on Saturday and Sunday mornings. Granted, many
are married, but a lot aren't. Grab the newspaper—depending on
the sort of guy you want to meet, determine ahead of time if it's
the *Wall Street Journal* or *New York Post*—order a venti, and sit

down. If an interesting guy is in earshot, comment on the incredible story about the rising price of coffee beans.

Join an activity club.   Every town has some sort of activity clubs such as ones for biking, skiing, or hiking. They schedule events, which are often geared specifically to singles. Even if they are not, since singles are comfortable traveling in these organized groups, there will usually be a number of them on a trip. This, once again, puts you in touch with people with whom you share an interest. It's also not a bad way to spend a weekend. Look for these clubs in your local newspapers or online, or call local bike and ski shops for information.

You can meet guys while walking or jogging through a park or along a bike path. An added attraction? Take your dog with you. He will be irresistible to many men.

Say yes to every invitation.   This is crucial for two reasons: One, you never know whom you'll meet—Roseanne, a single mom with two sons, met her future husband at a party—and two, if you consistently turn down invitations, they will eventually stop coming. It can be challenging going alone to a neighbor's cocktail party or to a dinner party with three other couples, but the alternative of sitting home and stewing is simply not acceptable. Even if there are no single men at these parties, if you come across as the self-assured, attractive woman you know you are, the other couples will think of you as a potential fix-up.

Accept any invitation to hear a speaker or a politician. You'll have a ready-made subject to discuss with the other attendees, plus it's a very inconspicuous way to meet someone. Gladys, a divorced mom of two teenagers, was introduced to a man with whom she eventually had a long-term relationship while attending a charity function.

Not to be maudlin, but twice I attended funerals where, in one case, I met a man I went out with and, in another, a woman fixed me up with her brother. You just never know.

Entertain at home. If the invitations aren't coming, give them out yourself. Rather than face a long holiday weekend alone, plan a barbecue and invite your friends. Host an elegant dinner or cocktail party. Schedule a festive Christmas party with hors d'oeuvres and dessert. The more invitations you extend, the more you will receive in return. As a clever twist, invite all singles to a party and request they bring a friend of the opposite sex.

Pursue female companionship. Being single is always easier when you have other singles to hang out with. By getting yourself out there you will also meet other single women. They will expand your social circles. Judith says she has an active social life with her girlfriends: "After I divorced, married friends weren't interested in having me around. I pursued female companionship the way women pursue men. I went to a church singles group. I was as much seeking female friends as men." You seek female friends so you have people to relate to, but it's also not unusual to meet guys through them. A girlfriend who starts dating might fix you up with her boyfriend's pal or her brother or sometimes with a guy she used to date.

Bars and clubs. Cruising the bars and clubs may not be for everybody. This is where your having made friends with other single moms comes into play. It's much easier slouching up to a bar if a girlfriend is in tow. The downside here is that you know nothing about the guy who offers to buy you a drink. The upside is that a lot of women I know have met their significant others in bars.

Carol has always met guys in bars. She'll go with her friends to bars in upscale hotels and restaurants. A number of clubs in Philadelphia, near her home, cater to singles. Many of them have restaurants, so you can go with a couple of friends and have dinner without feeling you have to stand by the bar. Just get up several times to walk to the ladies' room, or go outside to use your cell phone. You need movement in these places in order to get around and meet guys. Melanie met her serious boyfriend by accompanying her single girlfriend to a local bar. Now she and her boyfriend get a kick out of going there as a couple.

Since meeting a guy in a *bar* takes on a connotation of reckless abandonment (i.e., drinking and pickup), it may be easier to tell your kids you met him in a restaurant. Also, unless you are wearing your soccer mom sweatshirt, you can't easily avoid the men who aren't interested in you if you have kids.

If you feel rusty about picking someone up or getting picked up in a bar, be aware that the scene hasn't changed all that much since the last time you were single. The biggest difference is that now "Can I buy you a drink?" can come from either of you. If you want to draw more attention to yourself, order some fluorescent, fizzling martini cocktail that just begs someone to ask you what you're drinking.

Have I Got a Guy for You!

You need to swallow some pride and get the word out there when you are ready to date. Then follow one important rule: Be eternally grateful to the matchmaker. Yes, do this, even if the date turns out to be unemployed, in love with his ex-wife, and smelling of an overindulgence of Old Spice. The reason your friends don't like to fix up singles is that they're afraid of making a mistake and incurring everyone's wrath. Let them know how appreciative you are and tell them, "What a great guy. It's too bad there wasn't enough chemistry."

Fix-ups are great because the date comes with at least some sort of pedigree, something that's missing in Internet dating or meeting a guy in a bar. And fix-ups are very easy to explain to your children, especially if they know the matchmaker. They can convince themselves that Mom isn't on the prowl. This date, they'll figure, just fell into her lap, a notion that may be easier for them to accept, particularly when Mom first begins dating.

One negative to a fix-up is if it doesn't work out, chances are that you'll be in each other's presence again, perhaps at a party at the home of the fixer-upper. Still, these are worthwhile dates. Turning one down is a little like shooting yourself in the foot while wearing Manolo Blahniks.

Elise, an architect, says she often meets guys through fix-ups: "I've probably dated over fifty people and some have been introductions through other people. A friend who works as a realtor fixed me up. She introduced me to a guy to whom she sold a house."

Many of my dates have been fix-ups, some of which turned into long-term relationships and a couple that never made it past that first cup of coffee. Either way, I still never miss an opportunity to thank the person who set us up.

> *There are countless opportunities to volunteer—political and social causes, highway cleanups. These are occasions to meet men while doing something worthwhile.*

Business and Pleasure

Forget about never mixing business with pleasure. Nowadays there are many ways to meet guys through business, and it doesn't have to be by encountering each other over the top of your cubicles. He might be the UPS man (you already know he has great legs), a client or customer, or a salesman who peddles supplies to your company. You just want to feel secure that your dating a particular guy won't ruin your professional status. In other words, if he's your boss or your employee, consider first what's at stake. Also when your relationship ends, it can be difficult still seeing the guy at the office. Julie, a pharmaceutical salesperson, and Sally, a banker, each had long-term relationships with men they met through work.

There are also many professional associations and out-of-office conventions or meetings that provide an opportunity for you to meet men. Elise, an avid golfer, has often met men, most married, through business-related golf outings. One day, though, she received an unexpected call from a business associate with whom she had played golf: "He asked me out to a black-tie affair. I didn't even know he was single."

Because so many jobs today require travel, it's not unusual to meet a man on a plane or a train or while eating alone in a hotel coffee shop. Judith, who travels for her job from Texas to New York, dated someone she had sat next to on an airplane during a business trip: "We have branch offices in each other's city. It worked out, even though it wasn't easy." Sometimes you will meet a guy on a business trip who is from your area, and facilitating dating is a lot easier. If you're planning a plane trip, ask for the middle seat—it increases your chances of meeting a single guy. And if you are on a train, put something on the seat next to you until a prospective catch gets onboard; then move it quickly.

Get Packing and Get Going

By looking in your local newspaper or going online you will find a singles event every week. In fact, you will find several. These can be attractive and nonintimidating ways to meet men. I ripped out an ad in my weekly newspaper for a "solo night" at a theater about a forty-five-minute drive from my house. The ad read, "No one to sit with? Got a reluctant significant other? Come to a wine, beer, and dessert reception for easy conversation." It then suggested that you might meet someone to sit beside at another performance. Here's something you can do alone and feel fairly comfortable. There are always parties, lecture series, movies for singles. Even if you fail to meet a potential date, at least you can have a nice night out.

Many more tour operators are becoming clued in to the number of singles out there with money to spend on travel and no one to travel with. You can now book a trip or a cruise devoted to singles. In fact, MatchTravel.com allows you to book a trip for singles online. Take advantage of the tour companies if you're nervous about traveling alone. Or go to an all-inclusive ranch in Wyoming, or a Club Med in the Cayman Islands, or the wine country (any wine country—California, the south of France, South Africa—will do!). And don't negate trips with your kids just because you're anxious traveling as the sole parent. As a single mom, I've traveled all over the world with my kids and have frequently encountered other single parents with their own children in tow.

Pray or Prey?

Open up any newspaper and you will find a list of single events that are religious by nature. These events have the benefit of being significantly less edgy than barhopping, and if a guy's religious preference matters to you, you've already checked off one of your priorities. It actually isn't unusual for women to meet potential dates in a place of worship. That's where forty-four-year-old Christine began her first long-term relationship. People tend to be friendly and not posturing in these venues and are easy to approach. Besides, your children will automatically assume, rightly or wrongly, that this guy is more trustworthy by virtue of your finding him in such a location.

These events are not necessarily held in religious institutions, and in some cities you can find the religious organization sponsoring a singles group event in a bar.

Seeking Mr. Right

Personals have been around forever, and even though my one-time-ever answering a personal ad led me to my failed second marriage, I know of plenty of women who found the man of their dreams this way. Personal ads, which have taken a backseat to the Internet, can give a responder a tinge of not being very up-to-date, presumably not very tech-savvy. The advantage to the newspaper or magazine ads, though, is that there is a lot of anonymity here, and if you are interested you will speak to each other by phone immediately. On the Internet, you often e-mail back and forth so often that any hope of a relationship fizzles out before you discover the squeak in his voice. You can also root out the men who aren't interested in dating a single mother by listing right off the bat that you have children. This gives the guys who reply an immediate check on the plus side.

Sandra answered personal ads a few times without much success before she finally turned to the Internet: "I once put an ad in a local newspaper. I got three answers and all were guys selling Herbal Life who wanted to get me into their pyramid." Oh well. It doesn't work for everybody.

Another advantage to personal ads is their prevalence and accessibility. They appear in your local magazines and newspapers, including the lofty *New York Times*, and the freebie rags that show up on your doorstep or in your mail once a week. The cost of placing an ad could run from free to hundreds of dollars.

Your Date on a Silver Platter

Dating services aren't cheap, but since they do a lot of the leg-work for you, including weeding out the men who reject your be-ing a mother, they can be very appealing. Sandra says she has paid between $500 and $1,200 for a dating service though it's not unusual for a client to spend $5,000 to $10,000 (and in several cases much more) for a limited number of guaranteed dates. Some services will admit their supply of middle-aged men is lim-ited. It's not that there aren't available single men; it's that, for their own reasons, men would rather scour the Internet, a less committed, more anonymous venue, than pay for a dating ser-vice. Men may also be more cautious about submitting to an ex-tensive interview, which dating services require, and revealing personal information such as salary and phone numbers.

So what have these dating services done to rectify the male shortage? They have targeted men where they can be the most effective—in sports sections of newspapers, for example—and given them deals for signing up.

You can find traditional dating services advertising online, in your local phone book, and in your newspaper. In most cases you will pay a fee for a specific number of fix-ups, often within no time limit. This is where you are expected to be patient. Sandra hears from her dating ser-vice infrequently; just when she thinks they've forgotten about her, she gets a call.

Dating services offer a lot of the same benefits as fix-ups, but for a hefty price.

There are many dating services with a slightly different bent, such as It's Just Lunch! This service bills it-self as "first date specialists . . . who arrange quality lunch dates for busy professionals in a discreet, no pressure setting." Depending on the franchise—there are sixty or so nationwide—you pay about $1,500 for an average of a dozen lunch set-ups in a year.

Christine joined It's Just Lunch! and although she admits she "got worn out" after nine introductions, "as an experience, it was worthwhile even though they didn't match me up with the right person. Most of the guys had really good jobs. If he's willing to pay $1,000 or more, he's not going to be a chimney sweep."

This service requires an in-person interview to talk about your education, background, hobbies, and goals, and it uses that information to select prospective dates. Your last name and phone number are safeguarded.

Great Expectations is a video dating service that has been around for so long I remember getting mail from it back in my twenties. In this service, you screen videos, photos, and the personal data of prospective dates. After you choose whom you'd like to meet, Great Expectations contacts him for you.

There are also online dating services, such as Drip.com, in which after you go online to select a prospective date, Drip.com lets him know you are interested. You do not e-mail each other. Instead you meet in a coffee shop. These aren't in every city yet, so check online to see if there is a location near you.

Together Dating has combined with the Right One dating service to form a service that mixes computer-aided personality profiling with old-fashioned matchmaking and consequently claims to have been responsible for thousands of marriages over the past three decades.

One unique type of introduction agency is the gourmet club. Eight at Eight arranges dinner parties for four men and four women, all single. For most gourmet clubs, you pay an annual fee, usually ranging from $100 to $500, though a few are free, and then you pay for your meal. Because Eight at Eight limits women to under age forty and men to under forty-five (only to capture more males), other gourmet clubs have sprung up for older singles.

The idea here is that meeting for a meal is fun and less intimidating. Normally four men and four women gather first for cocktails under the eye of the organization leaders, then settle down for fine dining together. The participating restaurants are accustomed to writing out separate checks for each diner as well as splitting the cost for any wine that's selected. If you're interested in someone at the table, a date can be arranged by the dating service. Some of these groups also arrange travel and theater events for singles.

These gourmet clubs, including ones that don't limit the age the way Eight at Eight does, can all be found online and include, but are in no way limited to, Dinnerintroductions.com out of New York, Singlegourmetchicago.com in Chicago, Atlantaupscale singles.com out of Atlanta, and Singlegourmetdfw.com in the Dallas–Fort Worth area. Look online for "single gourmet" and you will very likely find a group in your area.

Matchmaker, Matchmaker

Granted, matchmakers conjure up images of *Fiddler on the Roof*, where love—though not always true love—is delivered to your doorstep by the local practitioner. He or she does everything for you. The matchmaker attempts to find the perfect man and then arranges the introduction. And for this, while you might not be giving away your dowry, you are paying dearly.

Gentlepeople, based in Boston and run by matchmaker Zelda Fischer, can charge anywhere from $6,500 to well over $25,000, according to the company. Gentlepeople advertises its services as a "Nationwide club for marriage-minded professional men and women" and includes clients in twenty-two states. If you are interested in privacy and discretion and money is no object, then a matchmaker will work diligently to find you a mate.

In addition to Gentlepeople, more modern-day matchmakers have sprung up. In New York and Los Angeles, for example, matchmaker Samantha Daniels of Samantha's Table not only sets up clients with other clients but, if need be, will introduce them to nonclients who show up in her social, cultural, or professional circles. She then arranges a meeting over drinks rather than put them under the pressure of sitting through a full meal. Initial consultation and placement in her database can cost a few hundred dollars while the actual introductions run in the thousands.

Like a lot of modern-day dating services, both Gentlepeople and Samantha's offer personal coaching to teach you how to act on a date.

Really, is there anything money won't buy?

Dating at the Speed of Light

Speed dating. What could we expect from a culture that devours fast food, enjoys lunch-hour face-lifts, and FedExes overnight to Tokyo? Remember all the times you've told your kids to just give that girl, teacher, boyfriend (you fill in the blanks) a chance? Now you have about five minutes to determine whether Mr. Right, the guy you hope to spend your entire life with, the man who will be stepfather to your kids, is a worthwhile match. No pressure.

As part of the speed dating process, you register to attend an event, usually in a bar or restaurant, and with the pace of musical chairs you spend a few minutes with one man before moving on to the next one. If you like a certain guy, you mark it down. If he likes you, the organizer will tell you and you can then slowwwwww down and actually go on a date.

To become proficient in this process, you have to know how to sell yourself in one minute's time and then give the guy the same opportunity to make his case. With a minute remaining—whew!—you get to sum up your lives. Obviously, critical information would cover what you do for a living, whether you each have children, and what your passions are. Keeping a chart so you can recall whom you spoke to is very helpful.

One of the original speed dating services, HurryDate, holds events nationwide. With this service, the women generally remain seated while the men spend three minutes with each before moving on to the next table. The problem with a lot of these services is that there are not enough middle-aged people available to make a speed date event worthwhile for that age bracket. This may change as more consider this option, though.

The website Pre-dating.com lists the speed dating events across the country. You can go online for a date and place, and it claims that you will meet about a dozen people in less than two hours. You pay about $35 per event, which is restricted to a particular age range. Each month the age range changes—it can be twenty-two to thirty-two one month and forty-five to fifty-five the next. Check online for details.

Everybody's Gone Surfing

The Internet has become such a popular place to find a date that in the course of a month about forty-five million people visit at least one online dating site. And more than half of these are looking for a serious relationship. Also, according to the *Wall Street Journal*, those elusive men the dating services are searching for make up 60 percent of the visitors to online personals. If you've been nervous up to this point about entering the dark, infinite world of the Internet, get over it. Meeting a guy on the Internet is really no different from meeting a guy while walking your dog. In both cases, so long as you have a decent pooper-scooper, you'll be able to determine whether he's worth a relationship.

Sandra belongs to six Internet dating sites, to which she devotes about an hour, total, each week. She logs on, checks a thumbnail sketch and picture of a particular guy, and then, if she's attracted, goes to his page. She can scroll through a long list of guys, eliminating her rejects in a matter of seconds.

"He's wearing sunglasses—I hate that," she says. "I wouldn't call this guy; he doesn't make enough. Five-nine, 150 pounds, okay, so he's thin. I like an entrepreneurial type. This one's a 'gemologist.' That means he works in a jewelry store. This one is a 'Labrador lover.' That means he LOVES his dog. This one says he 'gets along well with animals and kids.' Yeah, how well does he get along with women? Oh, and here's one pictured with his mom." At the end of an hour's examination, she comes away with two guys to e-mail. She hears back from one, and they get together. Over the years, Sandra has dated dozens of men she has met on the Internet.

It's not as intimidating as it seems, and once you log onto a site, the particular website will walk you through it. Even if you hardly use the Internet, you'll find dating sites to be surprisingly easy. Most of the sites ask you to post your profile, which includes your biographical information and a photo (you'll need a digital camera—try a disposable one if you don't own one). You can then view thumbnail sketches of prospective dates. However, if you want to contact a man or read his full profile, normally you have to become a member for a fee of about $25 a month.

In an attempt to preserve her privacy, Elise, who began surfing the Internet after several friends found boyfriends online, doesn't like to send a picture of herself. This limits the number of men willing to respond to her query. If you are hesitant to post a picture of yourself, you will definitely reduce the number of guys who respond. You expect to see a picture of the guy, so understand his reluctance to call you if you don't give him the same opportunity.

Again, keep in mind that the number of potential matches you receive will be determined by the qualifications you plug in.

The more requirements you place on the men you want to meet, the fewer the matches that will turn up. Give some thought to your list of priorities and see if one might be dropped. You don't want to restrict your search.

Only two matches showed up when Sandra added a height requirement of over five-eight. I ask, would you turn away Michael J. Fox, five-four, or Tom Cruise, five-seven? She plugged in an income—over $100,000. Again, I ask if you would turn away a brilliant, interesting college professor making $85,000. She specified education—a college degree or higher. I ask—last time, I promise—would you consider Bill Gates, who never graduated college, an intellectual inferior?

Age is another qualification about which you should consider being flexible. Don't think you are limited to men your age or older or that your age is a turnoff to most guys. Yes, there are fifty-year-old men advertising for women twenty to thirty, but would you seriously want to date such an insecure guy? In reality, you will find younger men interested in dating you, and you shouldn't reject them just because they were pledging a fraternity while you were working on Wall Street.

> *"I don't want a really good-looking guy. I want him to wake up and say, 'How did I get someone so good-looking?' They don't have to develop their personality and psyche when they rely on looks." —Elise*

Elise has found that "most of the guys I know don't have a problem with how old you are." I found the same to be true and, in fact, have dated more men a few years younger than me than men my age or older. AARP, the organization for people over fifty, conducted a singles survey in which it found that 34 percent of women aged forty through sixty-nine date younger men.

Theoretically, if you relax even one of your requirements, you open up your world to some potentially great guys. There are some impressive five-foot-six single men out there who slip past everyone's radar screen.

When you do finally connect with someone, don't drag out the e-mails between the two of you for too long. Rather, after one or two, suggest you meet for coffee. And there are precautions you can take just as you would in meeting any unfamiliar man for the first few times. Never give your full name either in your profile or as part of your e-mail address. When you're ready to talk on the phone, block your number by first dialing *67. When it comes time to give him your phone number, give him your cell rather than your home phone. It's harder to trace. And don't meet someone without talking to him on the phone. You can tell a lot from his voice.

Short of hiring a private detective, you can try to confirm a guy's profile by plugging him into search engines like Google or calling his place of business to make sure he works where he says he does. You can also log onto Bigyellow.com, which offers a reverse directory that allows you to type in his phone number and secure his listing. You might feel like a snoop but you'll also feel a lot more reassured.

It goes without saying that you should meet the first couple of times at a public place, like a coffee shop, and not at either of your homes. In fact, Sandra never specifies where she lives and instead only reveals the name of the county. You can also ask a friend to call your cell phone at a prearranged time to make sure you're doing okay.

One dating site, Udate.com, offers the following recommendations to its customers: "Common sense precautions should . . . be taken when arranging to meet someone face to face for the first time. At Udate your real identity is never disclosed to any other member or anyone else." Really, this is helpful information whether you meet a guy online or at the gym. Until you get to know someone a little better, you want to keep your private life to yourself.

The most popular site, Match.com, claims success among its million members with hundreds of thousands of matches resulting in finding a lifelong partner. Although Match.com is a general site for singles of all ages and backgrounds, other dating sites cater to niche audiences. ScienceConnection.com, for example, serves singles interested in science and nature, RightStuffDating.com is for graduates of top colleges, and BlackPlanet.com introduces African-American singles.

Some sites, such as eHarmony.com, claim to find you a better match by requiring you and the potential dates to fill out extensive personality profiles. Although your choices are fewer, they are more tailored to you. Another site, Greatboyfriends.com, guarantees that every man listed has been vouched for by a best friend. SpringStreetNetworks pools the personal ads of some 200 publications while Relationships Exchange is a network of many of the personals sites. There are even sites to help you write your profile such as E-Cyrano.com or Profiledoctor.com. AARP will also help you write a personal ad.

Among the most often heard negative reactions to online dating is that the system fails to keep out married folks. In fact, according to a Nielsen/NetRatings study, about 10 percent of Internet users of dating sites are not single. It's also not uncommon for prospective dates to tell little fibs, particularly about their age or height and weight. One other negative is that because a selection of dates on the Internet seems endless, sometimes if you settle for I'myours.com, you could be plagued by the notion that a better guy might have turned up.

All of that aside, if you are looking to meet men, the Internet is a great place to search. There are lots of dating sites available, and the number keeps growing. Following is a sampling of some of the most popular ones:

Amigos.com—For Spanish singles

AnimalPeople.com—For singles who love their pets but are looking for a person

BlackPlanet.com—For African-American singles

ChristianCafe.com—Single Christians looking for love

ChristianSingles.com—For "marriage-minded" single Christians

Craigslist.org—Clearinghouse for personals for all singles

Date.com—For all singles

DreamMates.com—For all singles

EHarmony.com—Requires singles to fill out extensive questionnaires

Epersonals.com—For all singles

Friendster.com—Meet as friends, not necessarily as dates

Gay.com—For the gay community

GreatBoyfriends.com—All the men listed are referred by other people

Jdate.com—For Jewish singles

Kiss.com—For all singles

Match.com—The largest site for all singles

Matchmaker.com—In-depth profile required for all singles

MuslimMatch.com—Service for uniting Muslims in marriage and friendship

Nerve.com—Edgy, sexy urban singles

Personals.Salon.com—For all singles

Personals.Yahoo.com—Another very popular site for all singles

PlanetOut.com—For gay and lesbian singles

RightStuffDating.com—Must be a graduate of a top college to be a member

SassySeniors.com—For senior singles

SeniorFriendFinder.com—Seniors finding friends and dates

SeniorsCircle.com—A site for seniors

Tallpersonals.com—For tall men and women

✳ ✳ ✳

Regardless of the steps you take to begin your dating process, make sure you go through them with optimism. Believing "It's a man's world" and "All the good ones are married" is not only crippling but false. Looking for love can make you very vulnerable as you handle rejection from men, who, for that matter, you only went out with because you felt sorry for them. The way to keep insecurity from creeping into your psyche is to feel good about yourself, first and foremost.

Though you may feel cautious, don't be afraid to level with your children about how you've met a man. You'll probably let it slip anyway, and as they become more accustomed to the process you are using to meet a guy, they will become more accepting. Without actually becoming intimately involved in your search process, they might even get a kick out of the unusual ways you meet dates.

Enjoy the search and all that will happen along the way—you'll meet so many interesting men and women who will become good friends, you'll experience foods and hobbies for the first time, and you'll have something to tell your friends when you sit up at night with a bottle of cabernet sauvignon and the Entenmanns chocolate cake with the marshmallow icing. Don't let dating drive you until you are burned out. There will always be single men out there looking for love just as you are. Don't believe me? Just browse online.

CHAPTER THREE

The First Date:
A First for You and Your Kids

Preening in her new lavender underwear while contemplating a closetful of expertly tailored but boring business suits, newly single Gladys agonized over her first date in twenty-five years. She had no idea what to wear, where to go, or who would pay. When a friend suggested she feel romantic and treat herself to a teddy, Gladys was thinking stuffed animal.

She dug out her dog-eared copy of *The Sensual Woman*, dabbed on expensive perfume, applied new makeup, and carefully slid her first-ever issue of *Cosmo* under her bed like a teenaged boy hiding *Playboy*.

All suddenly single women can relate.

After years of feeling more at home in the bathroom than in the bedroom and being so clueless as to think streaking meant she was out of Windex, Gladys had to update her knowledge of social rituals and take stock of herself.

Rewarding dating experiences are preceded by a boost in self-confidence, an improvement in attitude, and, if necessary, a refinement of appearance. Whether you exercise, enter therapy, order a subscription to the *New York Times* (at least read the front page), change your hair color, or undergo plastic surgery, if you feel good about yourself, mentally and physically, dating will not only be life altering and life affirming—it will be a blast.

Don't let a negative reaction from your children to your first date dissuade you from going on one. It's a first for them, too, and time, honesty and patience (especially yours) will ultimately result in their adapting to this change in your life.

Taking the Plunge

Look at your first date as experience. No attachments, no commitments, no pressure. Remember Sandra's first date, Slugger? It was their first and last date, but he left her curious and anxious to begin dating in earnest.

A first date signals to you, as well as to family and friends, that you are ready to move on. But preparing for one can be nerve-racking as you deal with issues never before experienced, such as telling your kids, and then knowing where to meet, what to wear, and how to act. Once you actually get together with your date, you will be surprised how relaxed you'll feel. All your trepidation and anxiety over the prospect of dating will vanish. You'll realize he's just as unnerved as you are, and you'll approach every subsequent date with more self-confidence and excitement.

In anticipation of her first date, Gladys let her thrice-married girlfriend drag her into Victoria's Secret to liven up her wardrobe. She then set her up with a colleague.

"You'll like him," her friend told her. "He's just a little bit younger than you."

"How much younger?" Gladys asked.

"Midthirties. Not to worry: I told him you were in your forties."

"But I'm not," an exasperated Gladys responded as she re-called the fiftieth birthday party her ex-husband had thrown in a last-ditch effort to keep the marriage together.

"Don't worry. You look it."

A nervous Gladys, who in the end shunned the suits for jeans, only to find her youthful date in a business suit, struggled to keep up the pretense that she had witnessed Woodstock in a documentary rather than in person. It was their first and last date, but it gave Gladys the confidence to move on, and the next time she met a man at a charity event, she was a pro.

First dates come from all sorts of sources, as I discussed in Chapter Two, so be open to the possibilities.

Gladys's was a fix-up. Melanie met her first date in a bar. Christine's first date attended her church. Julie, a pharmaceutical salesperson, met her first date through work. Cass's first date was both a coworker and a neighbor. And Diane, a realtor, was newly separated from her husband when the landscaper who had worked at her home for years became a comforting shoulder.

"Before I got separated I was ready to be with another man," Diane says. "I let my heart lie dead in my chest for years. I am feeling sexy all of a sudden and I know that I have to find someone. Bill has done work at my home and my kids know him." Bill turned out to be such a superb first date that he and Diane married two years later.

> The most difficult moments of a first date are the awkward first and last minutes—the introduction and the good night.

Christine's and Cass's first dates both evolved into long-term relationships that ultimately ended when they realized the man was a poor choice as a lifelong partner. In Christine's case, the breakup thrilled her three daughters. "He was so nice the first year," recalls Christine. "But then he became emotionally abu-sive. The kids never liked him."

While their mom's dissolved romance pleased Christine's daughters, it disappointed Cass's kids. They had grown to like the man, who had no children of his own and often took them boating or to a game. Even when Cass planned to remarry, she continued to allow her sons to see her old boyfriend a couple of times a month.

Like these women, you never know where a first date will lead, sometimes to marriage, other times directly to your cell phone so you can call your girlfriend, who will invite you over for some Phish Food and commiserate with you about your spoiled evening.

Regardless, it's important to keep an open mind about this date. He doesn't necessarily reflect the other single men you will meet. When my first date told me he was unemployed and that he admired his ex-wife for marrying better the second time around, I knew that I wouldn't go out with him again. But I am grateful to him for asking me out.

I had to start somewhere.

Whaddaya Mean You Have a Date?!

Of all the steps you take in preparation for your first date, none is more crucial than informing your kids.

Ah, the kids. That's what's different from the last time you set out to date. It's not your parents waiting up for you anymore. It's your rebellious, surly teenaged son, who demands to know why *Mom* doesn't have a curfew.

And while the prospect of dating feels natural to you, make no mistake about what your kids are thinking. Fourteen-year-old Jeff speaks for most children when he says, "It's weird that my mom is dating." And twelve-year-old Caitlyn finds it "embarrassing when Mom has a date and I have a girlfriend over."

But don't keep the first date a secret for fear of repercussions from your kids. Gladys did. She lied to her son, telling him she was meeting friends for dinner, and was surprised to find him waiting up for her when she came in at 1:30 in the morning. Nonplussed, she had to stumble through a weak explanation.

Julie chose to conceal from her kids her first and subsequent dates with Brett until one day she realized she was in love. Now what? Her kids had never given up hope that Mom and Dad would reconcile. After all, they had no knowledge that either was dating, much less had fallen in love with another person. Not knowing how to tell them, Julie decided to bring her children to an office picnic, where she knew they'd run into her boyfriend. Despite being introduced to him as "Mom's coworker," the kids could tell immediately something was up. They felt embarrassed and betrayed. They started out on the wrong foot with Brett, who, after the next several years of this intense and tumultuous relationship, finally ended it with Julie. Her kids were delighted. As was Julie, now believing she had dated too soon after her divorce when, in her words, she "wasn't whole yet."

As intimidating as is the prospect of telling your children you are ready to date, there is no substitute for honesty and direct communication. "There are no secrets in a family," warns psychologist Beatrice Lazaroff. "Kids overhear a phone conversation between Mom and her girlfriend. They see her dressing up. You're kidding yourself if you think there are secrets."

It's easy to mistake your kids' being engrossed in a rerun of *Friends* with their being uninterested and unaware. They aren't. They will notice if you wear makeup when you usually don't. They will notice your talking on the phone, quietly, with the door shut. They will notice your new clothes, your whiter teeth, your giddiness. So save yourself some anxiety, and level with them about going on a date.

Lazaroff suggests that you sit the children down and say, "Dad's gone and you two are the most important things in my life. Just as you have other friends, Mom has other friends, too, like Susie. But Mom wants to have male friends, too, to go to the movies, to dance with, to have a drink with. "

A single mother enjoying the company of a man is normal and natural. If your husband died, reassure your kids that no one will ever replace Daddy, just as the birth of your son didn't replace your love for your daughter. In both death and divorce, you can't tell your kids enough times that no man will ever take their place in your heart.

But sometimes, despite having the best intentions, you get caught unprepared. You haven't considered yourself quite ready to date when you meet someone unexpectedly. He causes you to think, and you go for it.

When I got my first phone call from the man I'd met at that bat mitzvah, I wasn't sure what to do. I couldn't very well tell him to hold on while I went and had a heart-to-heart chat with my kids about "Daddy's gone and I'm still young and . . ." So I accepted. Needless to say, my kids were surprised when I told them I had been asked out on a date. I explained that the man was a friend of a friend, which, in my mind, cleared him of being an ax murderer or serial killer.

Noah, six at the time, was enamored of the other men in our lives, like my girlfriend's husband, Mark, who took him to basketball games, and our friend, Arnie, who climbed on our roof to change the outside floodlights. So Noah reacted ambivalently about my going on a first date. He opted to meet the man, Marty, and then within seconds of his arrival immersed himself in a video game. Debra at age ten was aware of how a date could evolve into Mom's remarrying. She insisted she was fine with my going out—which I'm not sure I believed—yet she preferred not to be home when he arrived.

The moral here is to recognize that your children will process your dating at their own speed and, until they accept it, will have little interest in joining in on your fun. You have nothing to gain by forcing your date on them. Be honest and be respectful of their feelings. Then let it go. A decision to go on a first date is yours. A decision to involve them with your first date is theirs.

In Roseanne's case, she was apprehensive about telling her sons she was going on a date. They were still riled over their parents' divorce and refusing to give up hope they'd get back together. Rather than upset them with the news she was dating Robert, she told them she was going out with girlfriends. For months, she carried on clandestine meetings with Robert at the end of her street.

The deception continued unimpeded until Roseanne discovered she had fallen in love. Now she had to break the news to her boys.

Extricating yourself from a lie is much worse than telling your kids the truth in the first place. If they trust you, they'll be more accepting of your social life.

"I've met this very nice man I'd like you to meet," she told them.

"Do we have to?"

"Well, yes."

"What about Dad?" they questioned her.

"You know we aren't together anymore."

"But you still love him, right?"

Anticipating this line of questioning, Roseanne responded, "Things change. Dad and I love you two very much. But Mommy also really likes this man named Robert. He really wants to meet you."

"Us?" They were surprised. "He knows about us? We don't know anything about him."

In answer, Roseanne explained that she had been reluctant to introduce Robert to the two most important men in her life until she was certain of her feelings toward him. She didn't want her sons to become too attached to him in case it didn't work out. Her boys, both under ten, gradually accepted her explanation and ultimately welcomed Robert.

In Julie's case, her children, particularly her eldest, distrusted Mom for lying to them about her dating. They were flabbergasted to learn she was in love. When her roller-coaster relationship with Brett ended a few years later, Julie found herself trying to re-build her children's confidence in her ability to pick a mate.

This unforeseen and abrupt falling in love experienced by Roseanne and Julie frequently happens when women resume dat-ing following a hapless marriage or the loss of a beloved spouse. Even though your sane, unimpassioned self says, "I will know be-fore I fall in love and there will be plenty of time to ease the kids into it," your emotional, impassioned, hormonally charged not-having-been-in-an-intimate-relationship-for-quite-some-time self can find the distance between not dating and being madly in love a stone's throw.

If you've been up front with your kids from the outset, then you can lessen the shock this sort of news will cause. Honesty doesn't guarantee your kids will be happy but it does reduce the anger they might feel.

Your children, regardless of their age, gender, or birth order, will react to your dating. The eldest child may shoulder responsibility for the younger siblings and for Dad and may fear betrayal and a loss of attention from Mom. She, as in Julie's daughter's case, may be the last to come around. In some families the older child serves as Mom's biggest supporter. Christine's eldest daughter, already dat-ing a steady boyfriend, related her own situation to her mom's.

A younger child can just as easily react in a number of ways, from feeling displaced and abandoned to feeling indulged by the attention of a new male figure. You have to read your individual children and then be open and direct with them.

If your children act annoyed when you tell them you're going out, ask what is really bothering them. Is it that they miss their father? Or that they fear Mom won't love them anymore? Are they embarrassed about their mom's going on a date? Chances are they'll answer yes to all three questions. You know how to reassure them about the first two. The embarrassment? Bring up examples of people you know, especially the parents of their friends, who've been divorced or who've remarried. Their kids had to adjust to their parents' dating, too.

Often a child will feel threatened by a date, fearing the man will take her place. Judith's eleven-year-old daughter hated the thought of her mom dating. "You don't need a boyfriend, you have me," she told her mom.

"You are right," replied Judith, a corporate executive who had divorced after a twenty-year marriage. "I don't need a boyfriend, but I want one for doing things I don't do with you."

"Like what?"

"Like going to an R-rated movie. Going to a bar and dancing. Speaking about religion and politics." Judith watched her daughter slowly warm to the concept.

Until your kids reach that point, they can take you on a wild ride.

Your going on a first date does not always mean to them that others will follow, including ones that may end in marriage, blended family, and Mom and Dad never reconciling. Now you are dating and your kids, whether they like it or not, must begin to accept it.

When his mom started dating, eighteen-year-old David says, "I was pretty young, only eight. I was more or less trying to figure out what was going on between Dad and Mom. I didn't understand what was going on. But I think I thought she was trying to find someone to relate to; to have some sort of relationship."

Ryan, also eighteen, says he has gradually adjusted to his mom's dating a variety of men. "It's her thing," he says. "It doesn't bother me a lot." My son, Noah, agrees that he doesn't consider it a "big deal" that I date, now that he's a teenager.

But eighteen-year-old Molly, unwilling to share her mother's love and attention, viewed it as a blessing when, after her father's death, her mom put on weight and refused to date. Then, years later, her then-forty-eight-year-old mother met a rather needy thirty-four-year-old man and devoted all her time to him.

"It was so weird," Molly painfully recalls. "He was closer to my age than to hers. He was six-four and looked like Shrek!"

Incidentally, there's another lesson here: A man you might consider Brad Pitt handsome, your children are likely to see as looking like Frankenstein. Beauty is in the eye of the beholder. Thankfully.

Like all single moms, you instinctively hope that your children will support and encourage your beginning to date and will automatically like the men you date. But be careful what you wish for. Sometimes children are so desperate for a male figure that they become attached to every man you bring home. You're prepared to cut it off with the guy, but your six-year-old son likes him. Cass felt compelled to maintain a relationship with her first boyfriend for her sons' sakes.

Judith's son liked having a man around the house so much that he attached himself to his mother's dates immediately. He didn't understand that when Mom broke off the relationship, the guy wouldn't come around anymore.

Dad Versus the Date

Whether you are divorced or widowed, your former spouse will inadvertently play a factor in your children's acceptance of your social life. There's no getting around this one. Regardless of whether you are able to easily disregard their father in terms of your dating, your kids won't be able to. They will feel conflicted, especially if they love their parents equally.

Even if your husband died, his absence will affect your children's attitude toward your dating. Most kids who lose a father usually grieve silently but like knowing that within their smaller family they can still talk about Daddy whenever and wherever they chose. My kids could not fathom why I would bring another man into this mix, especially one who was short where Daddy was tall, or swarthy where Daddy was fair, or who had his own house and, heaven forbid, his own kids. Any man you date will have to become comfortable with your occasionally speaking about Daddy to your kids. If your kids bring up Dad in front of your date, don't shut them down. Include your date in the conversation: "My late husband used to put ketchup on eggs, too." Then slowly change the subject.

The issues a widowed mom faces may not be as clear-cut as those of a divorced mom. When you divorce, you put away the wedding picture. When you are widowed, you put it in a more prominent place. Then when you become serious about another man and feel it's time to gently remove the photo, your kids will notice. They may be angered and hurt by this seemingly callous act on your part. To help them, explain that you'd still like to keep the picture around, but it's not fair to your new boyfriend to know "I'm still thinking of Daddy when I am with him." Then ask your child if he would like to keep it on his dresser so you all can still look at it.

> *If your kids' grandparents—your former in-laws—disapprove of your dating, then don't ask them to baby-sit while you're on a date.*

And then there's the wedding ring. Before your divorce is final, you remove your wedding band. But when your husband has died, it takes some time to register you're no longer married.

You're also concerned about being disrespectful. Taking the ring off implies you're moving on, you're emerging from your profound grieving. I took off my wedding band when I began dating but not before, and to tell you the truth, despite a second marriage, three long-term relationships, and numerous dates, I still wear my engagement ring. Maybe I'd better explain this.

Rising into adulthood during Vietnam and the feminist movement, when I married in 1975 I shunned a fancy wedding gown, refused to register crystal or china, and proudly sported a dainty (translation: small) opal, my birthstone, in lieu of a diamond engagement ring.

By my tenth anniversary, I realized I had no nice dishes.

And no diamond ring.

My anniversary gift from Charlie the following year was a lovely diamond engagement ring, which I still wear on my right hand. I do this for two reasons: First, I didn't receive it until my eleventh year of marriage, and second, sometimes when I am approached by an unsavory guy I can pretend I am already committed.

Besides, it's pretty and I love it.

If you love your engagement ring or have a jeweled wedding band, you might want to take the stones out and have them made into a necklace. If you hate what the rings signify—your failed marriage—and you don't want to pass them on to your children, then sell them. If your former husband is the type who took the rings back as part of the divorce settlement, then thank heavens you're no longer married to him.

Divided Loyalties

Although divorced moms rarely are confused about whether to take down the wedding photo and remove the ring, they have to deal with the most challenging issue dating moms face: their children's divided loyalty between Mom and Dad.

Children of divorce are not only trying to accept a new man in Mom's life but feel stuck in the middle between their parents. This confusion is compounded by the nearly universal hope that their parents will reconcile.

"I hoped my parents would get back together," says Jeff, whose parents divorced when he was six and both remarried. "What kid doesn't?"

"It's classic," adds Lazaroff. "You can be forty-five and your parents are divorced and you hope they'll get back together."

Psychologist Barbara Noble, herself a divorced mom, adds that no matter how troubled the marriage, kids will always expect the parents to reconcile. "I don't know if the hope ever goes away. Life is much easier for the kids when the whole family is living under one roof. They don't have to worry about hurting anyone's feelings." More often than not in an intact family, the kids don't have to pick sides, while in a divorced situation, they do.

Cass was convinced that her going on a first date had prompted her kids to openly encourage Mom and Dad to reconcile. It wasn't until her ex-husband remarried that her sons finally accepted that their parents were not getting back together. It's a wonder there aren't more scheming kids like the ones in the movie *The Parent Trap*.

In Roseanne's case, the older child equated his mom's dating with being disloyal to his father. Her reconciling with her ex-husband twice, though briefly, further complicated the situation.

Like a lot of kids, eighteen-year-old Ryan says he often feels compromised and confused by his parents' divorce. Even though they separated when he was fourteen, Ryan never thought of them as unmarried, so when Mom told him about her first date, he expressed shock. "I never considered my mom single, so when she started dating, I was kind of wired. I wanted my dad to start dating to make sure it was an even kind of thing."

Ryan remembers how he felt learning of his mother's first date. A strange man called and asked for his mother by her first name. "Then she tells me she is going out with this guy if it's okay with me. I probably said yes. But I always feel sorry for my dad that he isn't moving on."

Understandably, it's a little easier for children to accept a divorce if both Mom and Dad are involved in new relationships. When you are, and your ex isn't, your child is liable to feel like Ryan.

This isn't fair to you. You have to explain that your dating has nothing to do with the reason your marriage ended. But once it did, both Mom and Dad became free to date. Tell your kids you'd love to see their father date but you can't force him to. Not only do you have no control over his social life, but he should have no "control" over yours by making you and the children feel guilty.

As women know, all too often the tables are reversed. Your ex-husband has begun dating or has remarried, and you, still running a household, shopping for school supplies, and organizing birthday parties, just haven't gotten around to it. Because the kids expect Mom to remain maternal and be their stabilizing force, they can be much harder on their mothers than on their fathers when it comes to dating. They probably won't like the bimbo Dad brings home, but they aren't in the least surprised to see him date. You, on the other hand, are expected to wash their soccer uniforms before you even think about going out.

Even though this double standard is unfair, it doesn't change the fact that you deserve a social life. Brian, now forty, remembers being confused when his mother started dating. In his adolescent mind it was inappropriate, bordering on immoral, for his mom to show an interest in other men. Even though young Brian accepted that his father dated, he viewed his mom's dating as a betrayal. Today, when Brian looks back on those years, he knows he treated his mom unfairly. One day your kids will understand, too.

Sixteen-year-old Lilly expresses pleasure that her dad remarried but feels bad that her mom hasn't been involved in a serious relationship. Like a lot of children of divorced parents, sometimes Lilly thinks she's expected to tattle to each parent about the other's social life.

Ryan agrees. He's forced into an uncomfortable position when his parents both pump him for information about the other.

David, whose mom has remarried but whose father doesn't date, says the pressure on him comes from his dad: "I'm always noncommittal when he asks me questions. My mom asks if my dad is going out, and I'd like to say yes because that would actually make my mom feel better."

You can't burden your kids with keeping quiet, nor can you burden them with spilling the goods. No kids want to be stuck in the middle between two parents they love. They don't want to feel like snitches because they've revealed details that ultimately will make each parent unhappy. The opening question "Is Dad dating anyone?" will always evolve into "Who is she? What does she look like? Have they dated very often? Do you like her?" Ouch. With every question you ask, you take a teeny notch out of your self-esteem. It's not worth it.

Putting your kids in the middle so you can find out what your ex-husband is doing is like being in sixth grade and getting your girlfriend to ask the boy you both have a crush on if he likes you. If he does, your girlfriend's crushed; if he doesn't, you are.

It's hard not to pry, but remember, your goal is to feel fabulous about yourself. If you do, you'll care little, or not at all, about your ex-husband's social life, and that will take a huge burden off your kids.

Not only must you and your ex-husband (if he's onboard) handle this side effect of your dating, but this is where your new boyfriend also comes in. He has to develop what Lazaroff calls "positive credits" with the kids. Help him out by not putting him and Dad in the same physical place, like at your daughter's field hockey game. It forces the kids into divided loyalties. So in the beginning, go it alone. Your goal is to support your child who has to play that game without worrying about whether Mom and Dad can be civilized in public or if the unattached parent is looking gloomy on the sidelines.

Noble adds, "How well a kid fares in divorce depends on the maturity of the two adults. Realize you are not going to be friends. If you were, you'd still be married. All you need to do is be civil."

When a first date evolves into a long-term romance, still try to keep your boyfriend out of situations in which your kids will have divided loyalties. You feel entitled to include him, and rightly so, but your wish is also to create a long-lasting and caring relationship between your kids and this new man. They need to trust this new person. Once they do, they will suggest he attend their games or other performances.

I'll Be at Teddy's

After you've told your kids about your dating, leave the decision about whether to meet this man up to them. You may have one child perfectly fine with answering the door and another who will choose that night to sleep at a friend's house. It's okay. Just give them time. But let them know that if you ever like a man well enough to date him long-term, you would insist they meet him. Most kids will say okay to this without really considering the possibility that it happen.

A newly confident, slimmed-down Melanie met a man in a bar shortly after her husband moved out. Her sixteen-year-old son was away at hockey camp, but her thirteen-year-old daughter, Brittany, was home. Melanie told her she had met someone and was going on a first date. She asked whether Brittany would like her mom to meet him out somewhere or have him pick her up at home. Brittany, supported by the presence of her girlfriend, decided to stay home and greet him. Melanie was astonished and overjoyed by how well Brittany reacted to her dating.

A week later, Melanie's son came home from camp and immediately displayed his displeasure about Mom's dating. "It's too soon," he argued. Melanie validated his concerns, agreeing it was "way too soon to date, but when a guy of this caliber comes along, you go with it."

Her son walked away without comment. The next morning he apologized to his mom. "It's not too soon for you to date," he told her. "I see you are much happier now."

Again, you have to go on with your life, not only for your well-being, but also for your children's. Your happiness affects theirs.

Most children would prefer not to meet the man on the first date and would rather wait to see if Mom dates him again. Brian can vividly recall meeting his mom's very first date when he was nine years old: "I was completely flummoxed."

Says psychologist Lindblad-Goldberg, "Your kids' meeting the adult is the same thing as your son's bringing a girl home. What does it mean? Are they dating or did the girl just give him a ride home? It's a different implication from Mom's meeting a guy and wanting to share her life."

While not insisting that your children meet and talk to your date, you do expect appropriate behavior, as you would in any social setting. Don't accept rudeness on the part of your children just because the situation might be awkward. And as to the guy, it's best if he reaches out to your kids without overdoing it. Kids like attention and recognition, but they hate it when the guy's trying too hard.

Before he arrives, discuss with your kids where you'll be and what approximate time you'll be home (make it later than you think so they won't worry), and tell them they can call your cell phone in an emergency. You need to establish their trust in you, not give them control. As you date more, you will gradually tighten up your accessibility so your kids don't call your phone too often or at inopportune times.

Dating Protocol

Once you line up that first date, you'll be faced with several decisions: Will he pick you up at home or will you meet him somewhere? Will you plan a dinner or just coffee? Will he pick up the check or will you offer to treat? Will you dress casually or wear business clothes?

Regardless of whether your children meet the man, they may witness your primping for the evening. So long as you're not putting on anything too seductive (it is your first date, after all), they'll be fine with this. Like Gladys, you'll probably obsess over your outfit. Make a decision based on the time of day, the location, and whether either of you is coming directly from work. If he is and you're not, dress appropriately so

> If he takes you to dinner, you may offer to invite him for a drink before or coffee and dessert afterward at your house.

you won't feel out of place. He probably won't notice your clothes as much as you will his. And remember, check out those shoes!

Next, you will need to determine a suitable meeting place.

Most women find that if they are familiar with the man—say, you know him from work or your daughter's volleyball team—it's okay to have him pick you up at your home. But keep in mind that when a guy picks you up at home, you are giving him a lot of personal information you may not want him to have yet—or ever, for that matter. If you meet him at a mutual location, such as a coffee shop or casual restaurant, the only information you get from each other is the type of car you drive.

You will take note of his. As he will of yours.

Dinner is okay for a first date if there's been some chemistry, either in person or on the phone, between the two of you. Otherwise, opt for a drink or coffee, something you can limit if you want to. You can always prearrange having a girlfriend call you just in case the date turns out to be dreadful and you need an excuse to take off.

"That was my baby-sitter. She's feeling sick. She's really sorry but she's asked me to come home."

If you are enjoying yourself and not looking to cut short this date. Your conversation could go like this: "Sorry, that was my sister canceling a dinner party this weekend. Her kids have the flu."

The first gives you a way to bow out gracefully, and the second lets him know your weekend plans have suddenly changed, making you available.

You get the picture.

These sorts of theatrics are particularly useful on a blind date, which honestly can be a little scary if it's your first excursion into dating. Although the more blind dates you go on the easier they get, as a novice you might feel a bit silly, having to describe yourself so you can find one another. You're somewhat fearful you'll run into your gossipy neighbors, or your ex-spouse. In my experience, meeting at a casual restaurant for coffee or lunch is the best. Get there early. Sometimes I stand near the entrance and watch the cars as they pull into the parking lot. Before I even meet him, I can check out his car.

This is not as shallow as it appears; it's rather necessary to ascertain background information on this man who might one day meet my kids.

A truck indicates he may have a hands-on job, like construction or landscaping. He's probably in great shape physically and not wedded to his gym. A Hummer indicates his desire to feel young and cool. He'll tell you about the successful business he started from nothing and will weave into the conversation his daily ritual at the health club. An SUV tells me nothing in particular. Except that he may not be all that environmentally conscious. Sorry.

If you are too anxious to stand near the door, or if you made a last-minute decision to wear heels and are thinking it was a poor choice, get seated. Tell the host you're waiting for a man; you have his description already, so use it. The host doesn't need to know it's a blind date, and he or she will unwittingly make your introduction for you.

So what will you talk about?

Conversation on a first date will inevitably turn to questions about your, and his, former spouse. You will want to know how long he has been divorced. Does he have custody of his kids? Or how long ago did his wife die? From what and was it sudden? You can volunteer the same sort of information about yourself. Anything else regarding his former spouse or yours should be off limits on the first date.

If you date a man who has never been married, you are entitled to question him without getting too personal. Ask him why "a great guy like you never got around to marrying." Give him an opportunity to explain, and then save your judgment for after you get to know him better.

Judith remembers hyperventilating before her first date. Incidentally, she's fine now and is currently dating so many men she needs a spreadsheet. She doesn't usually mention her divorce, but the guys generally ask.

And Gladys, who left her marriage after a long period of complacency, says she's constantly hammered with questions from dates about her divorcing for "no concrete reason. It's difficult for them to understand."

A man I know can't understand why no woman dates him a second time. He admits he brings up his ex-wife in a somewhat unfavorable light. Then, when his date responds empathetically, he turns defensive, arguing in support of his ex-wife. Huge flapping red flag. No one wants to date a person if he speaks about a former spouse except in brief, unemotional, anecdotal phrases.

If you've been widowed it can be difficult not to refer to your former husband wistfully, and if you've been divorced it can be challenging not to show bitterness toward your ex. Either situation is off-putting to a date.

What do you do when the check comes? Let him pick it up. If he ignores the check when it arrives, apparently expecting you to split the bill, at least you'll know he's cheap. If you don't like that quality in a man, well, look how much time you saved finding out. It's not a contradiction in terms to consider yourself both a feminist and a lady. And a guy who can handle that . . . wow! Plus, if the first date is likely to turn into a second and a third, you can and will reciprocate. You will invite him to dinner, order movie tickets ahead of time, treat him to dessert and coffee. If he's worthy of a second date, there will be ample opportunity to give back.

Although this is only your first date, it's helpful to think about how you would stop seeing a man you've dated only a few times. How do you tell the guy you don't want to go out with him anymore? I'm ashamed to say I've left many a message on voice mail. Though, in my defense, I always think it's easier for the guy, too, since he doesn't have to talk to me. My being open and honest doesn't necessarily make him feel any better.

> *"He pay? Absolutely. I don't want to start compromising being on a pedestal. I'm not reaching across the table. Most guys find that very offensive."—Elise*

Sandra, though, bluntly tells a guy she doesn't want to see him again. Take this year's New Year's Eve date. It initially seemed to have such potential. The guy insisted she drive to his house before they headed to his friend's party. Dressed appropriately in a snazzy holiday outfit, Sandra arrived at his home to find him in sweatpants. Huh? He wanted to be comfortable. At the end of the night he asked to see her again.

"No thanks," Sandra told him. "This isn't going anywhere between us."

"I'd rather just say it and get it done," she says. "I'll say, 'It's not going to work out.' Not 'me' not 'I,' but 'it's.' It's not the right fit."

I admire Sandra for her forthrightness. Though Carol and Sally say they, like me, tend to make up excuses such as "The next few weeks at work are really busy" or "I'll be away for a while." Of course, you could just stop returning his calls.

If you get to this point and your first date is not successful, as in Gladys's case, do not take that as a harbinger of future experiences. You're getting your feet wet. The more you go out, the better you'll be at conversation and at picking up the warning signs (like if he talks incessantly about his fourteen-year-old "Daddy's little girl" but has zero interest in your kids), and the more accustomed your children will become to your dating.

In fact, if they seem interested in your date, you should feel comfortable talking to them when you get home. But be calm. Neither trounce the date nor elevate him. Be matter-of-fact. Nice guy. Two kids. Divorced. What he does for a living. Where you ate. What you ate. It needs to feel ordinary and nonthreatening. By doing this you open up communication with your kids about this new development in your life.

Remember, this date may be for one night. Your kids will hang around a lifetime.

CHAPTER FOUR

Kids, Glorious Kids

Truthfully, I hate to date men with daughters. This is my own prejudice, I realize, but I have been on the other side of "Daddy's little girl" enough times to know that competing with her is like going on the Internet to buy Superbowl tickets. You'll never be first in line and you'll get frustrated just trying.

Now, having said that, I have in fact dated men with daughters who were positively lovely and with whom I got along great.

Those daughters were nothing like the fifteen-year-old one who repeatedly climbed onto Daddy's lap in my presence or the twelve-year-old who demanded Daddy stay home on Valentine's Day. Woman to woman, I got it. Even if he didn't.

I dated one divorced man who had a son and a daughter. When he spoke about his son it was with no interest (I liked the kid immediately). When he spoke about his daughter, his face lit up.

"I took her out to buy her her first bra," he told me. "A size A, can you imagine!"

Please, I was wearing one.

73

"I'm thinking of buying her a horse," he added, looking absorbed in his own vision of National Velvet with his precious princess on top, blue ribbons in her hand.

"Why?" I asked.

"Oh, I don't know. She just wants one."

Right, and my daughter wants a Lamborghini.

After years of dating I can now spot red flags when it comes to a man's children. There's only one thing that will impact our relationship more than his kids. And that will be mine.

We're mothers. We love our children and want nothing more than for them to be happy. They have suffered through the terrible loss of their father or a devastating divorce; we want life from here on out to be exceptional for them. All good things. And now we've gone and done it. We've introduced a man into their lives whom they didn't bargain for. Whether your kids remain silent or outspoken, you will constantly worry and wonder about what they are thinking.

And it doesn't matter whether they are six or sixteen; they will impact your dating in many ways.

The Dad Quest

All children want a father. The fact that my son, Noah, was seven at the time I met my second husband and so enthralled by having a man around the house certainly influenced my decision to get married. But I learned a valuable lesson: As much as your children want a dad, never jump into a relationship for that reason alone. You have to love, love, love the guy yourself. You have to view as endearing—rather than annoying—his squeezing the toothpaste from the top or leaving his breakfast dishes in the sink. You have to envision yourself growing old with him, the kids long gone.

The quest for a dad should never drive your dating. While I'm not minimizing the importance of a date's potentially becoming a great stepfather, be aware that focusing on this possibility can myopically cloud your own needs. How many divorced women admit that although their former spouses were lousy husbands, they were good fathers to their children? Obviously, a host of other reasons led to their divorce.

Besides, if your sole qualification for a man is that he'd make a good stepfather, what will you look for? That he's an equal provider? That he represents a missing father figure? That he'll deal better with your difficult teen than you will? That he'll take your son fishing? Where does *your* relationship fall in all of this? Is he also a good lover, a supportive companion, and a trusted soulmate to you? If these qualities are missing in your relationship, then you're giving up an awful lot just so your son can have a fishing companion.

Sometimes it is your child who pushes you into choosing a father for him rather than a partner for yourself. Judith has experienced this with both her kids. At fifteen, her daughter, Lydia, who never got along with her own dad, desperately craved a father in her life. "I keep thinking it's going to be better with her own father," Judith laments, "but it never is."

"But, Mom, I want a dad," her daughter cried.

"I'm going to find you one but I haven't found one yet. I'm going to keep looking. You'll need a dad even later."

"It's a heartbreaker," Judith says. "She sees me trying to find someone to coparent with."

Judith's son, a special-needs child, is also starved for a father figure. He wants his mother's dates to like him so much that he acts exceedingly well behaved—unusual conduct for him—in their presence.

Because her kids so obviously want a dad, finding a good stepfather is paramount in Judith's search for a partner, so much so it drives her dating. While there's no question that part of being a good husband to you is to be a good stepdad to your kids, don't let that be the only factor. If he is a bad husband to you, no matter how hard he tries at being a father, your kids will eventually dislike him. If you're unhappy, they're unhappy. It's that simple.

The Fine Art of Manipulation

Sometimes you have a child who doesn't intend to be manipulative but whose actions nonetheless control your relationship. Your child may be particularly needy, either for your attention or for the attention of a man. Maybe your child has a temper tantrum in a date's presence or calls your cell phone repeatedly or routinely complains of feeling sick before you leave for a date. Try to understand the reason for his or her behavior. Then tell your child something like "I recognize that Mom's bringing a man into the family is a new experience for everyone. But in time you will feel more comfortable with this. In the meantime, though, you have to allow me to get to know the man better to determine whether he is worthy of spending more time with our family."

If your child continues to misbehave and your talking with him accomplishes nothing, it will be advantageous for you to seek professional counseling. A child finding difficulty in accepting a parent's dating will benefit greatly from being able to confide in and receive advice from another adult.

Tell a manipulative child your cell phone will be turned off during dinner but give him (or, better yet, the baby-sitter) the name of the restaurant in case of an emergency.

It is tempting, and not always inappropriate, to ask your children what they think of a date. But be forewarned that such honesty often blows the lid off Pandora's box. You might find yourself trying to respond rationally to some irrational comments, such as "Does he always laugh like that?" or "He's a little weird." If you don't see yourself dating the man for much longer, don't even bother defending him. Their criticism may just be a matter of their needing to be reassured that this guy with the corny laugh will not replace them in your life.

"Kids don't want to share their parent with anyone else," Beatrice Lazaroff says. "And a lot of kids are manipulative."

In fact, even if only one of your children is recalcitrant, she can affect the entire household. Julie's eldest daughter hated Brett and consequently acted rude to him and openly annoyed by her mother. Because she served as a role model for the two younger siblings, she influenced the family dynamics. It was painful enough for Julie to face her daughter's disapproval, but when her two younger children followed their sister's lead, the stress resulted in her breakup with Brett.

Recognize that either divorce or the death of a parent leaves your kids with enough baggage to fill the cargo area of a 747. In a divorce, your children are conflicted by so many issues, it may be impossible for them to treat your date properly. If they get along well with their father, they will feel that sense of divided loyalty again. They aren't going to automatically endorse your new guy.

"Dad is always in the back of their minds," Gladys says of her kids. "It wasn't an acrimonious divorce, so they have no reason to want me to be with someone else."

"The hardest situation is divorce," Marion Lindblad-Goldberg says. "And a kid who feels protective of the mother is going to not make nice" to the woman Dad marries. And vice versa.

In divorce, Barbara Noble elaborates, there can be a fear of abandonment if one parent moved out. "What's to prevent this man from leaving? With widowhood, the extra component is safety issues. God forbid there's a car accident. Divorced kids don't go there as quickly. Initially, that's the biggest fear of children who lose a dad. There's still fear but it's not as pronounced as they get older and more self-sufficient."

I know that my safety had been my children's overriding fear when they were younger. If I went out on a date, the guy's car became an issue. A small convertible caused them sleepless nights, while a sturdy station wagon was a plus in my dating the guy a second time.

And although I was quick to dismiss their concerns, thinking my carefree response would be reassuring, in actuality I understood exactly where they were coming from. It more than once influenced who I dated. One guy, a divorced man who sported a showy handlebar moustache and held an interesting career as a sportswriter, frightened me so much as he blindly shifted from lane to lane on the highway that I ended our budding relationship. As nice a guy as he was, I had no intention of leaving my kids without a mother.

Many kids who are manipulative are not being so intentionally. They just don't know how else to handle Mom's dating. If they can possibly put an end to it and return normality to their lives, they will. Once again, you need to communicate with them: "I'm going to continue to date because I'd like to meet someone to spend the rest of my life with. When you get older, you will be happy and relieved if I am with someone."

They'll get it, eventually.

Using Kids as a Compass

I'm not always able to read my children's feelings toward a man. Even when they were younger, they rarely criticized my dates. Only once did either of them tell me not to date a particular guy. But my kids have a subtle way of dropping casual comments such as "I didn't think you liked facial hair, Mom." Or "But even you don't wear fur." Although I always take these remarks with a grain of salt, I think if they now—as young adults—told me to stop seeing someone, I probably would. Besides my own mother, there is no one on earth who has my best interests at heart more than my children.

Keep in mind that while your kids have some self-interest in the matter, they really do love you and want what's best for you. So look at yourself as being respectful and not submissive when you listen to their opinions. Their job, though, is to at least give a guy a chance.

Diane admits that if her sons, who loved her boyfriend Bill and welcomed him into her home, had insisted she stop seeing him, she would have. "If my kids, who are so perceptive, had questioned it, Bill wouldn't have been right for me. I think if it had come up, I probably would have looked very hard and deep into this guy I was dating."

If you have the courage to ask your children what they think and you aren't concerned that they will undermine your relationship with a man, go for it. Speak to them respectfully without forfeiting control. Your conversation could go something like this:

"Are you feeling you're getting to know Joe better?"

"I guess."

"Would you like to?"

"You're the one dating him."

"I know, but I'm also your mom and want to know how you feel."

"He's okay."

"He makes me happy. And he really likes you and your brother."

"Uh huh."

"You concerned about anything with him?"

"Well, just that he ignores me when you're not around."

"Really? Well, that's not acceptable. Maybe he doesn't realize he's doing it. I'll check it out."

Even if you dread hearing your kids' opinions, it's better to defuse a potentially heated situation early than to wait for a blowout. This comes as no surprise to you since your role as mother routinely includes stints as mediator, negotiator, and diplomat.

Melanie sees a practical side to relying on her children's opinions: "They could make my life miserable if they didn't like the guy and then I wouldn't date him. I wouldn't want them to be uncomfortable around someone I'm dating. It's too much work. It's work even when it's good."

Christine's kids were so concerned about the mercurial relationship smothering their mom, they didn't refrain from telling her the man was bad news. "I've always wanted their approval," she says, "because I don't think it's been easy for them." Once she ended that relationship, she was relieved they didn't tell her, "I told you so." Most kids won't. They will be so pleased you ended a bad relationship that they will have little desire to rub it in.

Elise's kids are older now, and so she feels confident they would tell her if they didn't like a man she was seeing. But would she end it? "It depends on whether I felt they had good reason."

While most moms, including me, say they would give up a guy for the kids, that should never be the assumed outcome. You have to believe that you, as an adult, know what's best for you. If you think a man is fantastic and you can't agree with your kids' negative reaction toward him, then maybe their dislike is based on their own needs. Does your being with him confirm that any possible relationship with Dad is over? Does your being with him mean your kids, in their minds, no longer come first? As valuable as your kids' opinions can be, they shouldn't be used as a gauge in your own judgment of your dates. You are the one who must assess everyone else's motives, needs, and perspectives in order to come up with an honest appraisal.

Lindblad-Goldberg says, "I feel so strongly that Mom shouldn't use her kids as a compass. No way should a mother decide whom she wants to be with based on what her kids think."

Lazaroff agrees that Mom has to stand up for herself. Have an honest dialogue with the kids. If the kids tell you they don't want you to date anybody, you need to tell them that you are entitled to a life of your own but will respect their wishes and not expose them to your dating. "If Mom is fair and honest but the kids remain nasty, then Mom needs to look at how well that kid is functioning. On the other hand, if Mom's a ditz and the kids have more sense—the guy is a loser, an alcoholic, like Dad—then maybe she needs to listen to them."

This is why you have to take a step back—several, in fact—in order to fully assess the relationship. You have to be able to discern whether your children are giving you valid advice or creating distraction. There is no question that if you put the relationship totally in your children's hands, you give them a power that guarantees your relationship will be doomed. Even when you were married to their father, your marriage suffered if you allowed the children to come between you. To permit that happening with a new man will erode any sort of relationship you hope to forge.

> *Your children are still missing their old intact family. Listen to, but don't rely on, their comments about your boyfriend. Consider the source.*

Regardless of your children's ages, they sometimes can't admit even to themselves whether they really like a man you're seeing. It's impossible for them not to be at least a little bit selfish and fearful of the changes this relationship will bring about. Encourage them to look at a man as the father of a friend. Would they like him then? Is he a nice, interesting, caring person? Is he pleasant to be around? Is he a good friend to you? To them? If they answer yes to these questions, then let them be. Continue with your relationship and slowly let your kids' comfort level rise.

Do the Kids Even Notice?

If your children seem ambivalent, don't for a minute think that translates into not caring whom you date. They do. Both my kids have warned me that because my second marriage was so dreadful, they have become more discerning about the men I date and less hesitant to comment. They didn't impose the last time, and look what happened.

"I don't think I'd tell you right away if I didn't like a guy," Noah admits. "You'd be able to realize it without my saying it. If I had to say something it could be too late. But I'm going to be more critical this time."

My daughter, Debra, agrees. "I definitely think I'd be less hesitant to comment now. But I believe the dynamic has shifted, not only because of the bad second marriage, but also because Noah and I are older. This time around I would be more vocal."

Ryan says he respects his mom's decisions but hastens to add, "She can't date a guy without my dating the guy. We're attached ball and chain!"

Molly takes it a step further: "If I hate the guy, Mom has to give him up. Yet I had a boyfriend once Mom didn't like, but she let me continue to see him. I know it's unfair."

You bet it is.

Right now you're thinking you can't win. You can, but only after you get past the bumpy part. The navigating will be left up to you. If your kids' concerns are over your happiness and not over their desire to have everything their way, that road will smooth over. Look at it as positive that your kid is willing to offer an opinion rather than silently harbor his worries.

David says he would have no qualms telling his mom what he thought of a guy: "I would say, 'It's whatever makes you happy.'" However, if he disapproves, he'll tell her, "But I'm not going to be happy with this guy."

A few years younger than David, and decidedly less reticent is twelve-year-old Caitlyn. She would definitely intervene if she had a problem with the man her mother was dating and would even go so far as to "split them up."

Her sixteen-year-old sister says she'd be more understanding about her mother. "It's her life—not mine," says Lilly. "I don't think I should tell her who to date."

But because she is younger, Caitlyn sees herself as being left stranded by her mother's dating: "It does affect me. I get stuck home alone. I have to cope with it." At this point in her life, it is all about her.

As she gets older and prepares to leave home for work or college, she will view her mother's dating differently. Right now she admits she doesn't understand what her mother is going through, but she does try to sympathize with her. Like most kids, when she develops her own life, she will become more concerned about her mother's loneliness. Because she is a young child, this is a difficult concept to comprehend. Young children think they will be with Mom forever and can't imagine themselves going off to college, much less falling in love and raising their own families.

Even Molly, who can be tough on her mom, agrees: "When I was little I'd tell my mom not to date. It's the two of us. Don't get married till I'm out of the house. It's always been the two of us. It's different now because I'm leaving home."

However, she hastens to add, "But if Mom became serious, I would still expect to be first. I'd tell her, 'That guy could drop you but I can't.'"

> Besides your kids, your friends and family will also feel you're spending all your time with him. Don't forget to include them in your life with phone calls, lunches, and "girls'" nights out.

What your children must understand is that no man who enters your life will ever cause you to "drop" your kids. If you have a child like Caitlyn or Molly who is worried about this, you need to reassure her. Not just with words, but with actions. Continue to find quality time with your kids even if you are immersed in a serious relationship. If you go away with your boyfriend one weekend, plan a special trip or event the following weekend with your kids. In fact, do this even if you think your children are handling your dating better than Caitlyn or Molly. You never know what they are really thinking.

Kids Adore Him, You Abhor Him

While you may enter the dating world thinking your biggest challenge will be getting your children to like the men you date, sometimes the tables reverse. You don't like the guy and want to break up, but your kids are attached.

My kids were supportive of my divorce because they were happy to see an end to that relationship. Yet my son was disappointed when I ended a long-term relationship a couple years later with a man he enjoyed hanging out with. I probably dated that guy longer than I would have because I knew it made Noah happy. In the end, you should neither choose a man nor continue dating him just for your kids.

"You've always been more focused on our needs," Debra tells me. "I hope one day you'll put yourself and your needs first in a relationship."

Cass continued seeing one man only because her sons adored him. When she eventually ended the relationship, he wanted to continue to see her sons. Cass allowed it.

"He came on in an open, kid-friendly way. Sometimes he stepped over the line and disciplined too much. But he got himself into the friendly uncle role and my kids responded well to that."

Once Cass planned to remarry, she began slowly weaning her boys away from her ex-boyfriend to enable them to develop a strong relationship with their new stepdad.

I admire Cass for serving her sons' needs while not compromising her own. If you can handle this and the guy is not going to
undermine you with your kids, then go for it. When a more permanent relationship enters your life, though, it becomes unfair to
this new man if the old relationship continues as it has. Put yourself in his shoes. If your new lover kept in touch with his old girlfriend through his kids and she had a relationship with them that
made it difficult for you to fit in, you'd want it to end.

Judith has cut off ties between her former boyfriends and her
children, especially her son. She finds it impossible for her kids
to appreciate her reasons for breaking up with a particular man.
One such relationship ended because the guy became involved
with someone else.

"I couldn't explain that to them," she says. "The reason you
break up with someone is a concept that is too adult, especially
for my son. He says, 'Why can't he come visit? Be a friend?' He
doesn't understand adult relationships."

He Likes Your Kids
More than He Likes You: Ouch.

What do you do if the guy ends up liking your kids more than he
likes you? In fact, you get the sense he's dating you only to hang
out with your little boy. This can happen, especially if you date a
man who has no kids of his own. He may form an attachment to
your kids despite not developing strong feelings for you.

In the movie *Jerry Maguire*, the character Dorothy, a single
mom, deals with just such an issue. Her sports agent boyfriend,
Jerry, loves her son more than he loves her. "This kid's amazing,"
Jerry tells his client, Rod Tidwell. Himself a child of a single
mom, Tidwell chastises Jerry: "A real man wouldn't shoplift the
pooty from a single mother."

For much of the movie, Dorothy laments, "I've got a great guy and he sure loves my kid and he likes me a lot and I can't live like that."

Neither can you. It's wonderful that he loves your child, but if you want a permanent relationship, he needs to love you, too. *Jerry Maguire* ends with Jerry realizing how much he loves Dorothy, and they all live happy ever after. But then, that's Hollywood.

Mr. Dad

If you think a relationship could develop into something long-term, don't delay meeting his children. How he acts toward them gives you insight into a part of his character you otherwise have not seen. You want him to be a good father, a doting, caring man, because then he is more likely to treat your children well.

In the beginning, don't be too judgmental of his children in how they treat you. This is new for them, too. If they have a mother in the picture, especially one who is still single, you may mean an end to their parents' ever reconciling. His kids feel as anxious about this as yours do.

That fifteen-year-old who sat on her father's lap eventually stopped doing that as she became more at ease in my presence. Frankly, I was more bothered by her father's failure to tell her it was inappropriate, especially in public, than by her actions. I understood she wanted me to recognize she would not be replaced in her dad's life. And I knew that when she finally had a boyfriend of her own, she'd stop devoting all her attention to Dad.

A man must take responsibility for his kids and how they affect his relationship with you. A more cowardly dad may continue to keep your dating secret, giving you less opportunity to meet the kids.

"He needs to inform his kids that he's dating," Lazaroff says. "It's the same thing as with mothers. He has to slowly introduce the woman to the kids. The same ground rules apply to the man."

It may be your job, though, to be the facilitator. If this relationship appears to be long-term, suggest you get together with his children. But don't have the kids meet each other yet. It's tempting if you think you are falling in love to expedite the entire "happy family" portrait. But such attempts usually backfire. The children, yours and his, are still many steps behind you and your date in terms of accepting their parents' dating.

However it comes about, don't fear meeting a man's children. They can affect your relationship in a positive way. Remember, you already know how to be a good mom, so you will be able to relate to his children on the same level you do to your children's friends.

> When you meet his kids for the first time, bring them each a little something. It shows your interest in them right off the bat.

If you have a twelve-year-old, you're probably pretty adept at communicating with twelve-year-olds and everyone younger. You've already raised kids that age.

When you meet them, act polite, but not overly so. Ask them about school or their sports team. Speak as if you know something about them, but not everything. (She'll be annoyed that Dad told you, a virtual stranger, that she got her ears pierced!) Try something like "I heard your volleyball team won its last two games. What team did you play against?" or "I took my kids to the latest Harry Potter movie. Have you seen it yet?" Ask questions that show interest and relevance. Don't ask them if they've read any good books lately.

Even if you think the meeting is going along swimmingly, I guarantee you the man will be watching every move you make. He'll be oblivious of his kids' kicking you under the table (really, most won't), but he'll pick up on the subtle tones of your voice and every indication of affection you display toward his kids.

Though Brett was a bad fit for her, Julie found his son to be a wonderful complement to the relationship. "He added to our relationship, especially since I didn't have my kids those nights," she says. When her relationship with Brett ended, she continued to miss his son.

So look forward to meeting his kids. And give them an opportunity to gradually feel more relaxed in your presence. Remember, these kids are going through what your kids are. And they may be some other single mother's children.

Impact of Pets—No Joke

You think your kids, his kids, your ex-husband, and his ex-wife are the only living beings weighing in on your dating? Then you've forgotten about Fido.

I dated a widower who had a perky, friendly terrier (read: out of control). He'd laugh when the dog would jump on me, put his frothy jaws on my navy wool pants, and bark when I sat on the sofa in his favorite spot, which was wherever I sat down. I wouldn't have minded any of those reactions so much if the same man hadn't kicked my cat.

Now, I understand not everyone likes cats, but he could have at least understood my point of view. Any thought of a permanent relationship with this man meant getting not only our kids to get along, but also our pets.

A few summers ago I saw the play *Sylvia*, which ruined things for me. There is a line that says to be wary of a man who names his dog after a woman. Subconsciously, that is the only woman in his life.

At least the widower's terrier was called Poker.

However, I dated another guy with a dog named Nicole. Before we'd leave his house for a date, he'd always go up to Nicole and kiss her on the top of her head, then turn and look sadly as the forlorn mutt whimpered over being left alone. Honestly, there is just no way to compete with that.

I dated another man whose four pets—two dogs and two cats—were so old he hated to have me back to his house for fear they would have thrown up or urinated in his absence. After a few months, I realized he was afraid to be alone with me. See what pets can tell you?

All the kids will observe how either you or your date responds to the pets. If your date is friendly and playful with your dog, he will find your kids much more responsive to him. The same applies to you with his pets. Remember, most pet owners, especially children, revere their pets. If you think your children don't like how your date treats you, wait until they catch him kicking your cat.

CHAPTER FIVE

Your Kids Aren't the Only Ones Behaving Poorly

I was in love; a feeling, an excuse, an act that suppressed my maternal instincts and caused me to shirk my parental responsibilities. I was reminded of being sixteen again and taking risky chances like sneaking out of my house to smoke cigarettes with the hugely popular girl down the street.

My children slept soundly in their rooms.

A few miles away, his children slumbered down the hall from his bedroom. He threw on a T-shirt and a pair of shorts, then stuffed his bed with blankets and pillows to silhouette his missing frame. It was the middle of the night—a steamy, hot summer's night, the kind that intensifies your thirst, merges all your senses, makes you delirious with sensual thoughts. Okay, steamy may be over the top, but bear with me.

I lay awake in bed until the gentle knock came. Swiftly, I climbed out dressed in my silk, spaghetti-strap nightgown, my well-worn, holey "Mom knows best" cotton nightshirt in a ball on the floor. After gingerly bypassing the creaky step, I opened my back door and nearly blew the moment as the rarely unlocked door first failed to budge.

We embraced. His kiss warm and salty mixing with the humid summer air. His arms intense and powerful as they wrapped around my petite frame. He caressed my back, my shoulders, and kissed me so passionately all thoughts vanished from my mind, all my nerve endings at high alert. I reached up and touched . . .

"Mom! Mom, where are you?"

Oh my God. What am I doing?

"Uh, I'll be right up, Deb. Go back to bed."

"Mom. What are you doing downstairs? It's three o'clock."

"Just getting a glass of water. I'll be right up."

I shuffled him out as quietly as I'd let him enter, closed the door, and hustled upstairs.

"You okay, Mom?"

"I'm fine, honey. I just woke up really thirsty."

With that I gave her a hug and walked her back to her bed.

I realized a few minutes later as I climbed into my cold, empty bed that she hadn't commented on my smelling of after shave.

What Happens to Your Good Judgment?

As good a mother as you deem yourself, when you begin dating your judgment becomes impaired. You worry about your children's behavior and don't even consider your own. You often don't think about how you've slipped from being Carol Brady to Peggy Bundy. You're giddy on the phone with girlfriends. You're acting affectionate with men in front of your kids. You're showing emotions you haven't displayed in years. Maybe not ever.

This out-of-body experience shocks you, forcing you to wonder just who this woman is, the one who's inclined to replace her age-old subscription to *Family Circle* with one to *Playgirl*.

Don't think your kids aren't noticing these changes in your behavior. You live in the same house, after all. You notice your children's subtle changes—like their talking on the phone longer or spending more time primping for school—so how can they miss your obvious ones? Your excitement before a date arrives, your snuggling with a date on the sofa, your rushing the kids to bed so you can have some quiet time to talk on the phone. None of this will be lost on your children.

Brian vividly recalls his mom's dating. And that was more than thirty years ago.

"I heard Mom on the phone with her girlfriends. 'What bar do you want to go to?'" he remembers overhearing. "I was in a huge state of denial." He couldn't assimilate this woman, on the one hand, raising him and his siblings and, on the other, going to bars to meet guys.

Julie understands this netherworld, a place where your maternal role conflicts with your sensual woman and it's anybody's guess which personality will arise at any given moment. Julie acknowledges now that when she took her kids to meet Brett without any forewarning, she was just "so tuned out." Her judgment was clouded at best.

Never assume that your child is sound asleep in her bed when you and a date turn passionate. That will be the one night she has a bad dream. Guaranteed.

Don't be hard on yourself. You have never before been in this situation. You spend so much time nurturing your children that there's no one to nurture you. Now suddenly there is. And you deserve it. You can try your best to control your adolescent behavior, but when you are in the throes of a passionate relationship, you aren't really thinking straight.

Unfortunately, your kids are, and they are observing your every move.

As mothers, we're so used to observing—and criticizing—our kids' behavior that we're not expecting them to criticize ours. Oh, but they will. And we'll probably give them reason to. It may be the only time in our adult lives that we resort to being teen-like again. The same behavior that our parents chastised us for in high school ("Your skirt's too short"; "You stayed out too late"), our children will now.

Revolving Door

Among the first actions your kids will observe is whom you are going out with and how often. They will notice whether the voice on the other end of the line is always the same or whether Mom's appointment book is filled with enough different names to man opposing football teams. A revolving door of dates can have its positives and negatives in your kid's minds. Regardless, don't involve them with all of these men, especially since most won't last past a couple of encounters.

Psychologist Noble says you're better off not bringing too many dates around unless a relationship is established. "You want to be careful about messages you give children," she says. "They don't need a series of men coming in all the time. Remember you are the role model."

Fifty-year-old Elise dated fifty to sixty men in the first few years after her divorce. Her three children, all teenagers, were aware their mom went out frequently. They viewed never seeing her in one serious relationship as healthy. They also appreciated their mother's honesty.

Elise says, "I never tried to sneak around or lied to them. I think my kids don't feel that I would ever dump them for some-one else. They don't have to fight for my attention."

There's merit, she believes, in her having dated so many men, finding the more she has dated, the more she has learned about her own likes and dislikes. "You interact socially and learn what is important to you in another person. You also learn what you are willing to compromise on or not."

This is a good point to consider. It's not unusual for women, and men for that matter—starved for physical companionship—to fall in love with the first person they meet after their marriage ends. Roseanne, Christine, and Julie all did. Roseanne's turned into a fulfilling long-term relationship, while Christine and Julie watched their feelings of adoration dissolve into intense displeasure.

The more often you date, the more men you will get to know. You will be able to draw a comparison, a kind of Pepsi–Coke taste test. A not terribly ambitious guy who dotes on you may look good if the overdriven, successful one is so self-absorbed that your interests run second to his, his kids', and his ex-wife's.

Besides, as Elise found, the more men she dated, the less threatening her social life was to her kids. They believed that so long as Mom juggled a variety of men, she'd never pick just one, settle down, and remarry. Her record? Eight or nine guys at one time. She uses a ledger to keep their biographical information straight.

"Different people fulfill different needs," she explains. Also, dating numerous men results in a surplus in case some don't work out. Elise admits that although she enjoys meeting so many men, she'd be happy to ultimately have only one special guy. "But it's taken me seven years to get to that point. I want a guy to be a complete person in and of himself."

Despite Elise's kids' approving of Mom's revolving door, your children might regard such a plethora of men quite differently. They might equate your dating a lot of men with your being frivolous—"Mom will date anything in pants"—or with your never being satisfied.

As my daughter, Debra, now twenty-two, tells me, "I think it's better for kids to get used to the idea of their mom dating. But

I don't think they should see a string of shady men running through their mother's life. To see her go out frequently, though, that's very healthy."

The most men I ever dated at one time was four. It wasn't by choice but a matter of "When it rains it pours." You're either date-less for months or feeling like Samantha in *Sex in the City*. But dating a lot of guys at one time is logistically difficult. There aren't enough nights in the week when you are also a mother. Your dating shouldn't preclude your being available, at least sometimes, to drive your daughter to the mall or your son to a party.

Judith dates four men, a number she considers less than ideal. She sees two in her hometown in Texas and two in New York City, where she often travels for business. The youngest is thirty, fourteen years her junior, while the eldest is fifty-two. Her trips to New York result in her squeezing in brief but quality visits with both men. It's complicated.

"I would like to have only one," she says. "But I want one who can be involved in my life. I see women who have a boyfriend who will do stuff with the family. The ones I find like that are long-distance."

The Guilt Trip

When Sally's daughter eventually learned her mother was dating, she became upset, imagining some man filling her space. Consequently, she laid a hefty guilt trip on her mom, who, as a full-time working mother, rarely had been able to participate in after-school activities: "My daughter makes me feel guilty by talking about how *good* moms pick up their kids from school." As a result, Sally couldn't bear to further disappoint her daughter by admitting she was spending some of her free time with a man.

Kids are masters of the guilt trip. And single moms are easy targets.

You feel guilty because your child has no father at home. You feel undeserving of any happiness until you've finished raising the kids. You never are finished, by the way. Your self-esteem may be so bruised you think you are to blame for everyone's troubles. You're not.

Try to take a step back and look at your children's behavior objectively. They might act out with anger and contrariness. Or they might respond in a more passive-aggressive way, claiming they're fine when they really aren't but refusing to open up to you. They are dealing with a fear of no longer coming first in your life and a belief that no man is good enough for you. A final blow is that they fear losing you. After all, they've already lost their two-parent family through death or divorce.

If you are open with them about your right to move on with your life, a development that does not mean leaving them behind, eventually they will come around. If you aren't honest, in the end you let them control whether you will date and, ultimately, whether you are content.

A soon-to-be divorced woman told me she was horrified by her teenaged son's reaction to her inviting an unmarried male friend over for dinner. When the man left the house, her son, in her words, "went ballistic." He wasn't prepared for men to be intimate with his mother. The woman decided to delay her dating a couple of years, until her son headed off to college.

Organize your time wisely for family, dating, and work so no one area suffers at the expense of another.

This young man effectively put the brakes on his mother's quest for a much-deserved romantic life. Your child may try to do this by showing his or her disapproval of your dating. This may manifest itself in refusing to acknowledge your dating or in making you feel irresponsible and unloving. Either way is not fair to you, nor is it behavior you should accept. Your refusing to date merely to satisfy your children encourages in them behavior that is made worse by your relenting.

The Kids' Behavior:
Miss Manners or Mister Smartypants

Just when you think you can predict how your children will act, they confound you by being nice to your date. Even kids who are displeased with your new social life will usually muster up all the manners you've drilled into them when confronted with your date. Sure, there are some kids who will humiliate you by being downright rude, but most will behave as politically correctly as is necessary. A quick hello, a handshake, and they'll vanish.

When Sandra began dating, her son was eight. He shook the men's hands, quickly checked them out, then ran to the basement. "When I'd come home from the date, he would walk like the guy or imitate him. He'd do something funny. He was just very tolerant."

Her daughter, on the other hand, acted discourteous. "When someone came to the house, she would run upstairs. She'd always ask if I was going to marry him. I'd always be honest with her."

Mom's entering the dating world drastically alters family life as it currently exists. Cognizant of this, your kids find it nearly impossible to be thrilled for you. Mom, in their minds, should be available not only to do the laundry but also to outdo Heloise in removing every last grass stain. A man alters your priorities. If Mom falls for that man, life in your household will be forever changed.

So give your kids time to come around and let them spend time with your date when they are ready to.

"Don't push them," encourages Noble. "Take your time. If your date comes over, let the children come down and talk a little bit. You'll create situations where they will bond."

Lindblad-Goldberg agrees: "I would favor having a natural response no matter what level of interest there is. If it's convenient for the guy to come over when your kids are there, then no big deal."

While kids can hold their own socially with their peers, they usually don't feel as capable when it comes to establishing a relationship with a man, especially one who has the potential to become a stepfather.

Gladys went out several times with a man with whom she ultimately had a long-term relationship. She chose a weekend she had custody of her son to finally introduce the two.

"Would you like to meet him?" Gladys asked her son.

"If you want me to," her son responded. "But don't leave me alone. Okay?"

"Okay," Gladys agreed, pleased the difficult task of asking him was over.

When her date rang the doorbell, her son opened the door. He shook the man's hand and introduced himself. Cordial but not overly interested, he then excused himself to go back upstairs. This is normal and fine. This scene may repeat itself numerous times before your child becomes comfortable having a one-on-one with your date.

After years of meeting my dates, my children have become adept at addressing them. I think they have been polite almost to a fault. One date was flustered when my then sixteen-year-old daughter and twelve-year-old son walked into my house and instantly put out their hands to welcome him. He didn't expect a woman's children to be so courteous and affable. Awkwardly, he stumbled over his words, introducing himself first as "Lawrence . . . uh, I mean, Mr. Jones . . . uh, call me Larry . . . whatever."

It was our last date. But, boy, was I impressed by my kids.

Carol and Sandra both found that the older their sons got, the less they liked their mom's dates. Men, recalling their own less-than-pure thoughts as teenaged boys, naturally distrust every boy their daughters bring home. This is the same thinking that causes your teenage sons to distrust every man Mom brings home.

Sometimes, as much as you hope your children will behave well in front of your date, they can't. They are just so conflicted. They don't want to disappoint you but on the other hand are terrified of this man's potential impact on your family.

As a single-parent family you are very protective of one another. "The biggest strength of the single-parent family is its closeness; that's also its biggest vulnerability as the children get older," says Lindblad-Goldberg. A divorce or the death of a parent glues the smaller family unit together. My kids fought like typical siblings until they realized how easily the family could break apart and how much they really mattered to each other. This closeness is one of the greatest benefits of being a single-parent family, but it's also the most distracting. These kids truly care about Mom, and with that comes incessant worrying and constant mothering (theirs of you). Do what you can by being patient, reassuring, and understanding. If the situation fails to improve, consider taking your family to therapy. Give your children an opportunity to vent to another adult without feeling they're disappointing you. An outside perspective can help all of you make changes for the better.

As an only child, Sally's daughter jealously guarded her mother's attention and remained fiercely concerned about her well-being. So the already guilt-ridden Sally chickened out about disclosing her dating, when in fact she could have used that mother-daughter closeness to bring her daughter in. When Sally went on a date with her daughter's math teacher and then reciprocated by inviting the man to a company Christmas party, her daughter was furious. When he came to the house, not for a tutoring lesson but to pick up his date, "My daughter got very upset," says a remorseful Sally.

In her case, more time should have been spent talking with her daughter about her intention to date, and she should not have brought a man to her home until her daughter had softened. She would have in time.

Beatrice Lazaroff warns that we need to be discreet about involving our kids, and that includes making an effort to find an appropriate rendezvous location or place to make love. "If kids are hostile to your dating, throwing a guy in their faces won't help anyway. If you have very needy kids, bringing the guy in isn't helpful either."

Before inviting a date to one of your children's events—for example, your son is playing in the school orchestra—talk it over with your child. Discussing it first develops trust between the two of you. It lets him know that you value his feelings and would never do anything intentionally to hurt him.

"I wouldn't just show up," says Lindblad-Goldberg. "Say something like 'Jim likes soccer (or in this case music). I thought it might be fun to invite him. What do you think?'"

Your questions are posed without your actually asking for permission. You don't ask if it is "all right" for Jim to come; rather, you present it as an idea.

Lindblad-Goldberg adds, "If he says no, I wouldn't do it. That's his world. Embarrassment is a big thing, especially in the middle years."

Ryan agrees. He was uncomfortable when his mom brought a date to one of his games. He worried about what his friends and their parents were thinking. It was embarrassing enough telling his friends that his mom was dating.

Gladys broke the news to her kids that her new boyfriend was going with them to a family friend's house for Thanksgiving: "It would have been different if it were just the four of us. It was okay because there were a lot of people spread out over three tables, and the kids sat together." But a month later, when she planned Christmas dinner, she chose to exclude her boyfriend, sensing her children were not ready to be placed in an intimate situation with him.

I have brought men to my kids' games, but not without their approval. Thanksgiving, a big family holiday in our home, is another story. If I have been involved in a long-term relationship, I will ask my children if they would mind my inviting the man to our holiday dinner.

"Events like Thanksgiving," my son Noah says, "I think it needs to be discussed. But I love when your boyfriend comes to my hockey game. I think it's fine. I like that someone has the balls to show up and isn't just taking my mother for a ride."

Public Displays of Affection

Even a child who allows you to invite a date does not want to witness any public displays of affection. Yet you've been starved for affection for a long time. Remember Helen Hunt in *As Good as It Gets*? She tells her mother she's been single so long, "which is probably why I make Spence hug me more than he wants to. The poor kid doesn't have enough problems; he has to make up for his mom not getting any."

"That's my mom. I just don't want to see or hear about it."
—Ryan, eighteen

This sentiment resonates with single moms. You remain a nurturing mother but you are no longer a married lover, so what do you do with all that displaced affection? You give it to your kids—that is, until a guy comes along. You are ready to burst. You sit close to him on the sofa, hold his hand walking through the mall, and kiss him soundly after he washes your dinner dishes. It feels wonderful and natural. To you, maybe, but not to your kids.

Julie remembers how uncomfortable she made her children after she finally acknowledged the existence of Brett and they all went to a Fourth of July party. "It was bad. I remember holding hands. The kids were disgusted."

As an adult I can appreciate her children's reaction. When my father died, my mother was fifty-seven. Two years later she met a wonderful man, who is now my stepfather, and the two traveled to Florida together for the winter. Charlie and I and our then small children flew down to spend a couple of days with them. My mother was in love. This woman who had raised me and who was married to my dad for over thirty-five years was acting like a giddy, love-struck teenager. Here I was in my thirties, a little repulsed by witnessing this side of my mom.

Imagine how your children feel.

Chances are that as a single woman you've been starved for affection for a long time. Along comes this guy who grabs hold of your hand while you're walking or puts his arm around you while you stand in your kitchen talking to your kids. It's a feeling of euphoria to be touched again by a man, and you deserve to enjoy it. Just consider where you are and who is with you. You know how uncomfortable you are in the presence of another couple kissing and fondling each other in public. Multiply that a few hundred times over to understand what your kids feel when they see Mom affectionate with another man.

"If my mom gets cuddly in public," considers Ryan. "I would have to say something because it's infringing on my life."

It has been years since a lot of these kids saw their own parents being affectionate, so now to see Mom in that role borders on revolting. Most kids will recall Mom and Dad kissing hello when either got home from work or an occasional hug after they performed a loving act, like cooking Christmas dinner or shoveling the snowy driveway. So now to see Mom affectionate is akin to seeing Mom as a stranger.

This discomfort in witnessing affection is not just reserved for Mom, though. Your kids feel similarly toward Dad and his new flame.

As sixteen-year-old Lilly says, although she accepts her father's remarrying, she hates when she sees him being affectionate: "I don't want to see it. They're newlyweds. My parents weren't affectionate when they were together, so it's hard to see Dad being affectionate with someone else."

Her younger sister, Caitlyn, is more explicit: "Yuk. I don't want to see old people like that."

Now there's a sobering thought.

Noah tells me he just assumes I hold hands when I walk with a boyfriend. In fact, not only would he find it more obvious if I showed no affection, but by my displaying it, he's more comfortable around me when he's with his own girlfriend.

You will be affectionate and you deserve to be. And your kids will have to get used to this because not only is it normal and healthy in a relationship, but you want them to bring this physical aspect to any of their future relationships. In their presence, do it gradually. You can begin by holding hands with your date when you all go out to dinner together, but keep some physical distance the first few times you bring your date into a situation that includes your children's friends. Their friends will be fine with your being physical, but it will embarrass your kids.

Kids Are Kids, Not Confidantes

Sometimes mothers think that if they involve their kids in the same manner they do their friends, their kids will feel more vested and consequently more supportive of a new man. You will be tempted to confide in the children, especially if they are teenagers. Don't do them any favors. It is easy to confuse their love for you with thinking they want to know everything there is to know. There is a limit on what you should tell them.

They should know details about the man you're dating—not his eye color necessarily, but his occupation, his interests, his hometown, his kids' ages. They should know details about your evening—not that you ended up back at his house, but the name of the movie or the restaurant. They should see how you dress for your date—not your fancy lingerie, but your flattering new sweater and skirt. And they should see your excitement—not your anticipation of a romantic night, but your happiness in going on a date.

Lindblad-Goldberg, who sees many single-parent families in her practice, says rather than confide in your kids about details of intimacy, find a close friend: "A woman should always have a best female friend or a really tight relationship with her sister, and that's who her confidante should be, not her kid. Kids have their own stuff. It's not that they don't love you, just that they have enough to process."

> It's okay to ask your daughter what she thinks of the outfit you're planning to wear. Even if she acts uninterested, she'll appreciate your valuing her opinion.

When I tell my kids something about a date that appears to be leading to a discussion about intimacy, even when it isn't, they stop me in midsentence with "Mom that's more than I want to know."

Admittedly, I am tempted to confide in my kids, who are now older, especially in my daughter, a mature and very wise adult. My son, Noah, tells me that he's always assumed I express more to Debra about my relationships than to him. And that's perfectly fine with him. He doesn't need to feel saddled with my love life. As Lindblad-Goldberg says, he has his own stuff to deal with. Incidentally, he also tells me that if his dad were alive, he'd probably feel more comfortable confiding in him as another man. "Still, Mom," he's quick to add, "I value your opinion on girls."

Eighteen-year-old Molly's mom confides in her frequently, viewing her only child as nearer to a best friend than any of her girlfriends. "We've always been very close," Molly says. "But if she wanted to talk about an actual physical relationship, I wouldn't want to hear it."

It's difficult enough for your children to think of their mother as a sexual creature, and even if they like your confiding in them so they can feel more involved in your life, they do not want to hear about your sex life.

"Those intimate moments are something you share with the guy," Noble counsels. "If you aren't comfortable with your sexual relationship, do something about it. Talk between the two of you or get out of it. But don't bring your kid into it."

Lindblad-Goldberg agrees, recognizing that while it's great that a woman wants to feel sexy, she shouldn't come home from the lingerie department and say, "See what I got" to her kids.

Like a lot of single moms, Judith has always had a special "girlfriend" relationship with her daughter. Although neither of them wants that to change, she recognizes there are boundaries to what can be shared. "She loves to dress me," Judith muses. "'Tell me you're not wearing those shoes!' Or I hear her tell her friends, 'My mom has a date and she can't dress herself, so I have to get off the phone now.'"

Lilly and her sister, Caitlyn, say their mom often confides in them. Lilly feels ambivalent about it, while the younger Caitlyn prefers it because it gives her the opportunity to react, and "I like her being aware of my opinion." Sometimes Caitlyn feels bad knowing that she has given her mom a hard time by disapproving of the men she dates. But, she says, it's only because she wants what's best for her mom.

"I would like for my mom to meet a nice, handsome, selfless, sensitive, genuine man who preferably doesn't have kids but really mixes well with my mom's personality and gets along with her well. They should be able to lean on each other for things and be very much in love."

From her mouth to . . .

In the meantime she'll continue to be a thorn in her mother's side—a watchdog, a protector. "I think when I do reach her age I will feel guilty. But for now I'm standing here."

Molly knows, too, that at some point she would be delighted if her mom found a great guy, someone other than Shrek. "He was such a loser. I think my mom is pretty great. She's fun. She's beautiful, and here she was with a guy so below her it embarrassed me for her. She really just liked having a companion, and I agree. I just wish it could be someone else."

✳   ✳   ✳

Your kids really do want you to be happy. They are just afraid of the unknown. They may have witnessed you in a lousy marriage already. They may have seen you grieve. They may have seen you treated poorly. They can't bear that. As soon as they can build up some confidence in their mother's ability to be happy, they in turn will be overjoyed for their mom.

Keep in mind that time will make all the difference in the world. Sandra has seen a change in both her kids through the years of her dating. As a young girl, her daughter was rude to her dates and her son constantly made fun of them. Now her kids are in their early twenties, living and working on their own: "When I go out on a date now, they say, 'Yeah!' They want me to be happy."

Christine's youngest daughter came a long way after initially expressing her fear of abandonment as a consequence of her mother's dating. She fixed her mom up with one of her teachers.

"This is something new," Christine says. "Number one, she's glad I'm out of that bad relationship, and two, I think she feels bad for me since her father remarried." Whatever the reason, Christine's daughter has slowly come around to accepting her mother's dating.

Give your children time to adjust. Let them see that it makes you cheerful, that you're looking healthier and more alive, that you feel confident. Don't push them by demanding they be delighted for you too soon. That would be behaving poorly on your part—easy to do while you're busy balancing motherhood and romance. Julie says she sees that now. Initially she didn't understand why her kids weren't pleased when she introduced them to Brett. She says, "I thought it was the best thing that ever happened to me and that my kids should be happy for me. I was frustrated. Why did they not want their mother to be happy?"

She adds knowingly, "Their lives were shattered."

When forty-year-old Brian was a young boy, he overheard his mom making plans on the phone with dates and with girlfriends to go to bars. His mom was oblivious of the effect this information was having on her eldest son. Not until he left his two younger siblings behind and moved in with his dad did she realize. By his senior year in high school, Brian had returned to his mother's home. She had given up some terrible relationships and had taken a long respite from dating. In the meantime she returned to school to begin a career as a bereavement counselor. When a neighbor's wife died, Brian's mother struck up a friendship which evolved into a romance and finally, a few years ago, a marriage.

Brian beams now when he talks about his mom's happiness. He adores the man she married.

CHAPTER SIX

❦

And You Thought Sex
Was a Thing of the Past

Maribeth judged the mothers who got caught in inappropriate moments as being reckless. That was before she met Wally. After a few dates a physical affection began to develop between them, taking on a life of its own, a breathless, out-of-control, "God-what-have-I-been-missing?" quality. Self-control gave way to lust.

One evening, Wally, confident Maribeth's children were safely squared away in bed, lifted her onto the top of the washing machine. In their hot-blooded, libidinous excitement, Maribeth's very naked butt hit the timer on the machine, discharging an excruciatingly loud buzzer into the quiet of the night.

A moment later a little voice said, "Mom?"

* * *

Think this can't possibly happen to you? Then you underestimate the passion you will experience when you reenter the dating world.

109

A powerful benefit to dating in your middle years is the awakening of a sexual desire either you didn't know you had or had forgotten sometime around the 3 A.M. diaper change. It will shock and delight you. And more than likely it will cause you to do things you not only never considered but, in your life as a married mother, would have viewed as irresponsible, if not indecent.

It will happen. And it will be wonderful—so wonderful that single mothers are caught off guard. It's neither their intention nor their expectation that they will deviate from snack moms into sack moms. But dating mothers often find themselves in compromising positions. If your kids catch you once, that probably won't stop you from having sex again, but it will make you extremely cautious. Rachel, a widow in her early forties, learned this the hard way.

For twenty years Rachel had stayed happily married to a man so particular about his home that he demanded his wife and sons remove their shoes upon entering, limit refreshments in carpeted rooms to bottled water, and keep their respective bedrooms as neat and orderly as a NASA space station.

His own clothing drawers were labeled.

But despite her husband's compulsion for tidiness and organization, he was wild and crazy in bed.

When he died following a long illness, Rachel busied herself caring for her kids, working part time in a gift shop, and maintaining a house that put Mr. Clean to shame. Sex was the furthest thing from her mind.

Then she met Neil.

One Saturday night the two accidentally brushed by one another as they squeezed onto a crowded dance floor at a nearby club. Just the gentle touch of Neil's hand on her shoulder as he apologized for the collision aroused in Rachel a sensation she thought had been suppressed forever. After all, she thought sex with her husband, like an airplane ticket, was not transferable.

Sex with a man who hadn't grown with her from her svelte twenties to her pregnant thirties to her varicose, cellulite-filled forties was, to put it mildly, terrifying. Instead, to Rachel's amazement, she found her renewed involvement in sex so exhilarating that, like a lot of dating moms, she sometimes forgot she had kids, three in fact, all boys, ranging in age from ten to fifteen.

One night Rachel was reminded.

She invited Neil over to eat dinner and watch television with her family. After her boys went to bed, she and Neil engaged in some sexually charged foreplay on the sofa.

Risky. Trust me.

In an effort to be discreet, Rachel suggested they slip into her bedroom and lock the door. Unfortunately, she hadn't calculated the residual effect of having been married to an obsessive-compulsive man.

"You'll have to get up and leave before my kids wake for school," she whispered to Neil.

"That's fine," Neil said as he fumbled with her buttons.

"Wait! Just in case they should wake, we'll let them think you stayed over in the extra bedroom."

"No problem," he told her, nibbling her neck as she pulled away. "What are you doing, Rach?"

"I'm just folding your clothes. Here, give me your shoes."

Neil watched his fastidious girlfriend put them into an orderly pile with his shoes on top, his wallet and keys stashed inside.

"You get in bed while I put these in the guest room," Rachel said.

Like a teenager, excited by the prospect of getting caught but not really for a minute thinking that could happen, Rachel dropped the clothes off in the room next door, shut that door, then scurried back into her bedroom.

At 5 A.M., the alarm clock went off as planned. The two lovers rolled over and kissed. Neil climbed out of bed and tiptoed into the darkened hallway. A few more feet and he would be safely ensconced in the guest room, where his clothes were lying, neat and tidy.

Then, suddenly and without warning, the hallway lit up. Like a deer caught in the headlights, Rachel's stark naked boyfriend came face to face with her startled fifteen-year-old son, who had just emerged from the bathroom.

What causes women like Rachel to cast aside motherhood for sex?

It's several things. For one, if you've been feeling somewhat frumpy and unattractive for years in a marriage, you now want to feel better about yourself. For another, women's libido peaks after their twenties, so chances are you're discovering new ways to have sex at a time in your life when your interest is high.

And third, you aren't dead yet.

The Prospect of Sex

Feeling good about yourself physically does remove some of the angst you may encounter anticipating sex. But most single women, regardless of their physical shape or the quality of the sex with their former husband, usually find sexual relations more gratifying as they age.

Your gynecologist can answer your questions about renewed sexual relations, birth control, and menopause. Make an appointment even before you begin dating.

After all, there are advantages to having sex when you and your partner are older. For one thing, the guy frets as much as you do about his physical appearance. He can suck in his chest for just so long, which does little for his protruding love handles anyway. He also has a fear of not performing as well as he did in his twenties. Viagra notwithstanding, he probably won't.

But by far the greatest advantage to having sex when you are both older is that neither of you sees as well anymore!

When you are suddenly single after years of being in a marriage, you might find yourself questioning your desirability. A cure is to look good and feel sexy. If you had a hostile divorce and you're looking for revenge against an ex-spouse, there's nothing more gratifying than to feel attractive. If he can do it, you can do it better. You haven't begun to hit your stride and he's already climaxed—in more ways than one.

Reaching this point of feeling sexy can seem daunting. All those years of not dating, psychologist Barbara Noble says, and then you're faced with "the whole experience of your doing the sexy role. After you've been a mom for so long, how do you become the woman in the Victoria's Secret catalog?"

"I was petrified," Roseanne says about the thought of having sex after her divorce. "It made me sick to my stomach. I didn't know how to act. I had no one to talk to. I had one single friend who'd sleep with anybody."

Like Roseanne, I, too, wished for someone to talk to about my renewed participation in sex. When I was first single in my late thirties, all my friends were planted in comfortable marriages. They could not fathom a woman their age entering a new sexual relationship—and enjoying it, no less.

"I can't imagine what it's like," said my very married girlfriend who times sex with her husband to coincide with each lunar eclipse. "I feel so sorry for you."

No need.

Admittedly, I was frightened, at first unable to imagine myself in bed with a man other than the one I had been married to. But eventually, I was dumbfounded—and pleasantly surprised—by my interest in sex. I hadn't felt so good about myself physically since I was in my . . . well, maybe never.

It's not that I was totally inexperienced, but I wasn't exactly sex-worldly either. Yet when you are older, you've already survived such extraordinary experiences as love, rejection, and child rearing. This gives you a level of confidence that evaded you in your twenties. It's an "Oh, what the hell. Why not?" attitude that permits you to try sexual acts that would have embarrassed you in your younger days. Is there anything that makes you feel more exposed or vulnerable than giving birth? Certainly nothing that will occur in your bed now.

As reluctant as you might be to face sex for the first time in years, you can, in fact, find it natural and fulfilling. Roseanne's dreaded first sexual experience turned out to be unexpectedly gratifying, as Robert whispered sweet flattering comments into her ear, reducing her anxiety.

As for Gladys, it had been so many years since she had enjoyed sex that she became very anxious after a soft-spoken, mild-mannered man stunned her on their second date by asking to sleep with her. "My jaw dropped. 'That's very interesting,' I told him. 'I don't think that's going to happen tonight but I'll give it consideration.'" After a few more dates, he stayed overnight at her place and slept in her bed, fully clothed. "He wasn't going to do that for too many times." Gladys finally relented: "It's always difficult to get used to other people's styles, but it went well."

Sometimes you will be surprised by how your first sexual experiences turn out. Melanie's first serious relationship after her divorce led to an uncomfortable sexual moment when her new boyfriend failed to keep an erection. But as she took on the role of comforting him, all her insecurities vanished. This can be a real leveler.

Elaine, a forty-two-year-old legal secretary, had been married twice, but her confidence as a sexual woman diminished when she discovered her second husband engaging in sex with women he met on the Internet. Immediately after separating from him she slept with two married men. "I was so hell-bent on being sexual after my divorce," she says. "Having an affair with the first and second married man was establishing my desirability."

With her two-year-old daughter sound asleep, she invited one of the men over and they had a "make out session into the wee hours of the morning." When her daughter was old enough to wander downstairs, Elaine swore off men.

She realized that her need to have sex was in revenge for her husband's transgressions during their marriage. When she understood that as her motivation, she took a step back, raised her daughter, and waited years to resume dating. Now she dates, feeling healthier about her attitude toward sex.

Like Elaine, when you find yourself single, sex may take on a purely physical or vengeful significance. Recognize that wanting to make sex part of your life again, regardless of your motivation, is acceptable and normal. After all, the Victorian era ended years ago.

Sex Buddy

With a feeling for revenge similar to Elaine's, Sally was eager to sleep with another man after her husband moved in with his new girlfriend. "I looked so damn good. This guy at work said, 'You're perfect!' As much as she enjoyed the sex, she worried all night that he would regard her water-filled bra as false advertising. Instead their strictly physical relationship lasted six months and in Sally's mind served as a much-needed experience. "He said, 'I'm using you.' I said, 'I'm using you, too.'"

He was Sally's first sex buddy.

A sex buddy is not for everyone, but it allows some women to engage in sex without the emotional attachment they might not be ready to handle. An ideal sex buddy is a man who places no demands, attachments, or commitments on your relationship. It's pure sex. Elise found it helpful having a sex buddy, especially one with whom she had little in common on a social, economic, or educational level.

"I could call him up, drink beer, and have sex and just talk for six hours," she says. "He knew that when I called him up that's what I wanted, and he never put reciprocal demands on me. He was available when I needed him."

The difference between a woman having a sex buddy and today's teenaged girls giving freely of sex is that the woman's date isn't getting something for nothing.

Since you only want men with whom you are developing a relationship to meet your children, it is unlikely you'll invite your sex buddy to Easter brunch. But if you happen to be in a situation where he meets your kids inadvertently, it goes without saying you will introduce him as anything but "my sex buddy." He can be a date, or a work colleague, or a friend of a friend. The irony here is that if you have teenagers or college-aged children, they are aware of their generation's practice of "hooking up," basically a one-night stand with no attachment or commitment. But the thought of Mom "hooking up" is more than any kid can handle.

The drawbacks of a sex buddy are similar to the drawbacks of hooking up. If you have an understanding that the connection involves no commitment and you find yourself falling for the guy, you will be devastated. You are also subjecting yourself to a man who very likely sleeps with other women, and that exposes you to the risks of sexually transmitted diseases.

Nevertheless, women like Elise find a sex buddy someone who fills a necessary void.

She insists, because she rarely sleeps with the men she dates—since "sleeping with a man still means something"—that she found satisfaction in having a sex buddy. He gave her pleasure, lent a sympathetic ear to all her troubles as a single mom, came and went at her command, and then to top it off was dynamite in bed.

Hmmm . . .

My Place or Yours?

More difficult than facing the prospect of sex is figuring out where to have it. Chances are that either you or he has kids at home, which puts a damper on using your bedrooms.

Elise says she has been fortunate in that she dated scores of men without ever inviting them to her house when her kids were home. She took advantage of the weekends her children stayed with their father, at least until they were old enough to drive and "surprise" Mom with an unscheduled visit.

Judith likewise refused to take risks with her children home despite being a "very physical person." Fortunately, she dated so many men without children she had ample opportunity to be intimate at their houses.

It's all about location, location, location.

Since I'm a widow, my kids have always been home with me. In order to invite a guy back to my house, I had to make extravagant arrangements for my kids when they were younger. You can only arrange sleepovers for them so many times without coming across like a mom anxious to get rid of the kids—and you are, to a certain extent.

Going to his house can be advantageous if his kids don't live with him. If he's widowed, they do live there, or if he has shared custody, they do some of the time. So when going to either of your homes doesn't work out, come up with some better plans.

- Rent a room. Seriously, there is nothing wrong with this. After all, you are entitled to be dating and you don't want to disrupt your children's lives by kicking them out of the house.
- Go away for a weekend. Even if it's only to a local bed and breakfast or to a hotel in a city close to your house, you

will have complete peace of mind that you will not be interrupted.

- Get together at either home during lunchtime, when the kids are in school. Of course, this works best if your kids aren't driving yet and can't show up unannounced.
- Find room in the car. I know this feels way too high school. But sometimes you'll find it happening naturally when the mood hits and you both realize you can't go home.

Caught in the Act

If you can't find a private location and you feel a physical attraction to a man, you can easily get carried away even with your kids upstairs. If so, they very well may catch you in the act. How in the world do you handle possibly the stickiest situation you will ever get into?

"Talk to your kid," Noble counsels. "Explain the passion. 'I've been single a long time. I'm sorry. It shouldn't have happened in front of you. Are you confused? Are you angry with me? I expect you to have feelings, and sure, it was pretty awkward. If you want to talk about it, I'm available.'"

If privacy remains elusive, deliberately schedule a "sex date" in a location like a hotel, where you can be undisturbed.

This is a very thorny position to find yourself in. Although you know better than to let this happen, it often does. Honestly, my children have walked in on a date and me when we quickly had to regroup and emerge from a spontaneous state of lust. It's a terrible spot to put your kids in. If you go there once, you'll never want to go there again.

Melanie now knows how this feels. She was certain she wouldn't get caught when she encouraged her new boyfriend to sleep over. She intended to wake him up at seven, hours before her teenaged children would see the light of day. The next morning he got up and headed downstairs to make coffee. As Melanie followed him out of the bedroom, she was confronted by her son.

"Why is he here?" her son asked.

"Why are you awake? It's seven on a Saturday."

"I have the SATs today. You forget?"

Melanie, a diligent single mom, now considered herself unfit for having had her boyfriend stay over and thoughtless for not remembering her son had to take the college admission tests.

"In a case like that you tell your child you had a date, and your friend got tired and slept over," Beatrice Lazaroff says. "You can't make it go away. It's there."

Carol worries about what her son may have witnessed when he was about two. "One time I was in the living room with a guy and we were just going at it. My son was asleep in the bedroom and he was a sound sleeper. I don't know what it was about that situation but I always wondered if he got up. He never would have said anything. I never would have known it. But I die at just the thought."

Cass had a similar experience when her younger son walked into her bedroom while she was in bed with her boyfriend, Phillip. "I screamed and said, 'Get out!' I got under the covers and continued to say something totally inappropriate. I had thought the door was locked. It wasn't," she recalls. "I just let it go and we never talked about it again."

If you have no impulse control, then at least try to create privacy, some boundary, just as you do in a two-parent nuclear family. You don't expect your kids to walk in on Mom and Dad, so create a place where they can't walk in on Mom and her boyfriend. It's better for them to be on the other side of a locked door.

Imagine how unsettled we would have been as children if we had walked in on our own parents. My older sister, Susie, still teases me for not understanding, when I was little, why our parents' bedroom door was locked at the oddest times.

First, try to chose a location that guarantees privacy, but if something occurs in the heat of the moment while you think your kids are sleeping, at least head into a room where you can shut and lock the door. And keep the noise down!

"There are no rules," Noble says, "but the mother has to think about the consequences of her behavior. They are looking at her as an anchor, and if she starts acting bizarre in their minds, they're going to feel insecure."

Sometimes your kids don't catch you in the act but find an embarrassing "souvenir." In fact, meticulous Rachel may have had the right idea. It's fairly common for a guy to inadvertently leave his boxers behind.

Impossible? How about this scenario? Your boyfriend sleeps over because your children are not home for the night. In the morning he sheds his boxers in front of the closed bathroom door before taking a shower. When he reopens the door to the bathroom, the discarded boxers remain where he left them but are now obscured by the open door. He dresses in clean clothes, and later that night your child uses the bathroom.

Before your kids return home from a weekend with Dad, do a Marine check on the bathrooms, the sofa cushions, and the bedroom, wherever telltale signs could be found.

I can hear it now.

Twelve-year-old Caitlyn never actually saw her mom in a tight situation with her boyfriend but did find his boxers. "And they were pink. Mom said he was changing his clothes. And I said, 'Yes sure, Mother.' I'm outspoken and I have a problem knowing about that stuff."

In reality, if your child witnesses in any way your having been sexually intimate with a man, she will be affected. We say kids are resilient, but some things remain burned in their minds. And witnessing a parent in a compromising position is one of those. I once dated a man who at forty-five years old remained bothered by having seen a pair of men's shoes outside his widowed mother's bedroom door when he was nine. And forty-year-old Brian still remembers his mom's sneaking a guy out early.

Sometimes, even if *you* behave with the utmost discretion, you're forced to deal with the fallout caused by your ex-spouse getting caught in a compromising position. Christine ran damage control after her youngest child stayed overnight at her ex-husband's. The eleven-year-old went to bed around ten with her father and his new wife sleeping in the neighboring room. She returned to her mother's house the next day visibly upset but repeatedly refusing to reveal the source of her distress. Finally, after much prodding, she told her mother she had overheard her father and his new wife engaged in sex.

Christine tried to give some explanation for the painful incident: "I said to her, 'They're in their own home. They are newlyweds.'"

"I understand," her child told her, "but do I have to listen to it?"

No, she doesn't. I don't like staying in a hotel and hearing some overheated strangers in the adjoining room. Even at my age, I am embarrassed as I take all three pillows and smother the sound. It's a wonder I'm not found suffocated the next morning.

Imagine how you would feel in Christine's daughter's shoes. You and your ex-spouse both have to be careful not to put your children in these situations. If your spouse does unknowingly, as in Christine's case, talk to him and urge him to address the incident with your child. It's always better to confront these embarrassing incidents with your kids, as difficult as that may be. You will help assuage any ill feelings or immature thoughts they may be harboring.

And remember, you are neither unfit nor thoughtless for giving in to your sexual urges while at the same time being a mother. You will learn from your mistakes and do better the next time. This is uncharted territory for women, and kudos to you for being the Susan B. Anthony for the next generation of single moms.

Sleepovers, without the Popcorn and Boy Talk

Getting caught in the act is one thing, but how does that differ from allowing a man to sleep over? In children's minds, sex and sleeping over do not necessarily correlate. Sleeping over is reserved for a man they think you'll eventually end up with. If you haven't begun dating yet, it may seem inconceivable to you that you would ever risk having a man sleep over when your children are either home or have access to a car and could stop home. The reality is that when you fall in love with someone or feel passionate toward him, you will take risks that in another part of your life would have been unthinkable.

Carol was in her late twenties when she first became a single mom. She frequently allowed men to stay over, at first when her son was only two, and then because it evolved naturally, she continued as he grew older.

"How many times did guys stay over? I thought it was okay at the time," she says. Years later, when her son was in college, she had become so accustomed to inviting men to stay over that she thought nothing of its impact. Her son, who for years had remained silent when men slept over, came home from school as she was about to go on a date and blurted out, "Just don't let him stay here."

His emotional comment jolted Carol into realizing for the first time ever that her son had been uncomfortable when guys slept over. She apologized to him and then vowed to herself to never again put her son in that position.

Sandra says she only permitted a sleepover if she was in a long-term relationship, and she was reluctant to have one if her kids were home. But one night her teenaged son came home early from his dad's house. "I said I was sorry and he said it was no big deal." Would she do it again? "No."

Men tend to be more lenient about having sleepovers even when their own kids are home. They generally don't suffer the guilt or feel the sense of responsibility single moms do. Children, too, are more accepting of their fathers than of their mothers being intimate with a date. This double standard is nothing new to single mothers, or to women in general, for that matter. A woman who sleeps around is considered wanton, while a man who sleeps around is considered lucky. How often do we say, "Boys will be boys"? But of course, in order to be boys, they need girls.

Although Julie would not let her first boyfriend, Brett, sleep at her house, she often stayed overnight at his while his son was home. "Brett thought it was okay. Yet I would not have him stay at my house with my kids. I felt uncomfortable. I thought it would hurt them because I wasn't married. One time I asked my son if Brett could stay over. He said yes, but I regretted it. It was the only time I ever made an exception, and a month later we broke up."

Don't think your kids are unfazed by a man sleeping over. Unless they are very, very young, they are affected by it. And you never know whom they are telling. Elise's former boyfriend, a schoolteacher, refused to stay overnight because he was so accustomed to his students' imparting stories about their mothers' sex lives that he didn't want to be the subject of a child's tale.

All of this is not to say sleepovers are inappropriate, but you do have to consider whom you are inviting over to share your bed and how to manage this without causing anyone to feel uncomfortable. It isn't a decision you should make lightly.

The ages of your children and the seriousness of your relationship will come into play here. Very young children may be accepting, but as they age, like Carol's son, they won't like it if casual dates stay over. Teenagers and older kids might be okay if you're involved in a very serious relationship. If you intend to be overt about his sleeping over, you need to discuss this with your older kids.

"Joe and I are getting back late tonight and I may let him sleep over. I hope that won't make you uncomfortable."

If your child is uncomfortable, he might suggest something like "Can't Joe just sleep on the sofa?" In this case, unless you're planning to marry or live with Joe, you may be better turning the sofa into his bed.

Roseanne allowed Robert to stay in her bedroom but not before locking the door and insisting that he hide in the closet if one of her kids came to the door. Her children still didn't know she was dating him, much less that he was hiding in her room. She woke him at 4 A.M. and snuck him out of the house. Months later, when it became clear to her children that she was going to marry Robert, they became accepting of his staying overnight in her bedroom. By that time, it felt appropriate.

Cass also waited until she was engaged to Phillip, when they told all their children that they would like to "wake up together." Upset by this news, Phillip's thirteen-year-old daughter ran up to her bedroom and slammed the door. Her father went alone to her room and gently informed her that their staying together was going to happen but it didn't have to be that night. When he and Cass chose to stay together a couple weeks later, all the children were fine.

It evolved naturally for Diane as well. Her boys knew her boyfriend because he had worked at her home as a landscaper. Unbeknownst to her sons, her ex-husband had frightened her by peering into her bedroom window. She told her boys that an unknown stalker had scared her and that her boyfriend, Bill, had offered to stay in the living room to protect them. They were so welcoming of him that in time, when he moved from the sofa into her bed, they thought nothing of jumping in bed with them in the mornings.

Lindblad-Goldberg completely understands a woman's desire to spend the night with a serious boyfriend. She fell in love with a widowed father of three girls. In time it became natural for her to spend the night. She wore flannels and bathrobes and didn't act seductive.

"I wouldn't do this with casual dating," she says. "I am not an advocate of Mom having strange men in the bed every weekend. It's reserved for a period when you are contemplating cohabitability or when the relationship is serious. Otherwise you make arrangements; instead of going to the movies, go to a motel. You need to be respectful. You say good night. Tell them if they need anything we'll leave the door unlocked." (Of course, not during sex.)

If a man fails to respect your refusal to have a sleepover, he's already missing the point that you're a mother.

Even if your kids say they are "fine" with your having a man sleep over, recognize their possible discomfort. You should be able to read your children well enough to ascertain whether "fine" means "What choice do I have?" or "That's cool." They might not be ready to conceive of Mom sleeping with a man. Give them more time to adjust to your serious relationship.

Just imagining their mom in that sexual role is difficult enough. Ryan says it upset him when his mom and her boyfriend went away together. "That was weird to me," he says. "They got a room. That's my mom. That's another guy. As a guy you're in the shoes of the guy so you know what it means. It's kind of scary."

You'd think Ryan's being "in the shoes" of the guy would result in his being more accepting of the situation. But kids have double standards for their moms, and what's more, they know it. Molly states unapologetically that although she'd not want her mom to have a man sleep over, she'd be thrilled to have her own boyfriend stay over.

If you decide to sleep over at a man's house, you need to consider the practical issues. Lindblad-Goldberg says, "Young kids can't be left alone overnight. You first go through having them stay overnight with a friend. I don't think you have to tell the kids what you're doing. With teenagers, who are so much more aware, I think you do not have to be explicit in what you say."

A sleepover handled secretly—as in Roseanne's case—is taking a huge risk. You may choose to hide him in a closet that your daughter ends up opening when she's looking for a sweater to borrow. It's different once your children accept that this man is likely to become their stepfather. Then sleepovers can be handled more openly. If the children are having difficulty, let them first see him stay overnight in another room or on the sofa. One night, have him fall asleep on your bed in his clothes and let your kids be aware of it. You'll be surprised. If your kids think this guy is in for the long haul, they may actually suggest you let him stay in your room.

Safe Sex at Any Age

For many of you, the term *safe sex* never arose in high school sex education classes, and chances are you engaged in sex in your teens and twenties, fearing an unwanted pregnancy but knowing little about sexually transmitted diseases. Now you are approaching or are firmly established in middle age. Do you have to worry about STDs? You know the answer.

You tell your kids to use condoms, and often you yourself don't. You think the other form of birth control you're using, such as the pill, is affording you all the protection you need. After all, you slept with only one man through the past twenty years. True. But have you considered whether he slept with anyone else or whether the man you are now dating, even if you are his first sexual relationship, was married to a woman who slept with anyone else? If you thought sex was out of your control when you were young, think of it now as a perpetually falling row of dominoes. You may know your sexual history and you may even think you know your current lover's, but anything beyond that is unknown.

The only way you can try to protect yourself against AIDS and other STDs is with a condom. It's awkward to tell a guy you've begun dating that before you'll engage in sex, he must wear a condom and get tested for HIV. But you will feel better beyond belief once you've done this. So will he. You should both get tested for HIV even if you've been monogamous. It's a show of faith as well as a guarantee your former partners weren't carriers.

Then there's pregnancy. If you're well into your forties or early fifties, you might feel fairly certain you can't get pregnant. You can. And women do. A full year after entering menopause you can become pregnant. (I know. I know. You thought this was the *one* benefit to menopause.) You must use birth control a year after your last period.

As a mother you have no problem insisting your kids be smart about sex. Now that you're back out in the dating world, you need to practice what you preach.

Mom as Hypocrite

Teenagers will be your most outspoken debaters, conveniently pinpointing the irony that what's unacceptable in their behavior is acceptable in yours. You have no curfew. They do. You can stay overnight with a date. They can't. You can have sex without a lecture. They can attend a lecture about sex.

As a good mother, you set standards for your teenagers. But because you are a single mom who dates, those standards meant to protect your child may come back to haunt you. You're forty. They're sixteen. How do you handle the fact that you are dating at the same time your child is or is about to? How do you enforce guidelines that they don't see you following?

First of all, approach this phase in your life as a single parent by automatically assuming that as hard as you try, as fair as you are, you can't win. Once you accept that notion, level with your kids about your concerns.

Their age and lack of experience demand a set of rules for dating different from the ones you follow. This fact will cause conflict and may ultimately require you to restrict yourself in ways that, though unfair to you, result in your sending the right message. If you don't want your children's significant others to sleep over in their rooms, then maybe until they're grown or away at school, or unless you're contemplating marriage or co-habitation, you don't have a man overnight in your room. It's not that you should be penalized but that you are trying to set an example.

You can handle this. You're a mother. You place self-sacrifice on the same list as food shopping, doing the laundry, and helping with homework.

Melanie admitted to her teenaged son and daughter that she was sleeping over at her boyfriend's and then regretted her honesty in confessing to her younger child that she had had sex.

"Mom, are you sleeping with him?"

"Yes," Melanie responded.

"Mom, you told us not to jump into sex with a guy."

"It's different. I'm forty-one. I know how to be careful."

I know I discourage lying to your kids about your dating but sometimes it is for the good of everyone to keep certain things private. Sex is one of them. In fact, even if your kids ask, they prefer not knowing.

"I was pretty sexually charged at sixteen," says Ryan. "I was hoping that was not what my mom and her boyfriend were doing."

Elise believes her daughter and her friends love all her dating stories. "Plus, they know I was having sex. It wasn't in their face. I am discreet and not promiscuous."

Still, her son worried her in high school when he became sexually active and wasn't "real intelligent about it."

Then a couple years later her desire to be an honest, up-front mom backfired. Her son was away at college when he called to say he was considering coming home for the weekend. Later that night Elise ran into a man she used to date and invited him back to her house. She called home to see whether her son had arrived. He answered the phone.

"I just ran into Wes. I'm on my way home with him," she said.

"What am I supposed to do?" her son asked, clearly annoyed.

"Go in your room."

When Elise arrived home she and her date retired to her bedroom. The next morning her son confronted her.

"My mom having sex is weird," he told her.

"It's okay for your dad to have sex but not your mom?"

"It's weird with you upstairs having sex."

"That may be, but I think it's weird that my son has sex."

Elise had been frank with all of her children in telling them that over the years she had had sex with a few of the men she dated. She didn't regret her honesty.

In your case, you need to know your own child and what he can handle. Despite my two young adult children's probably assuming I sleep with a man I am involved with long-term, I believe they would be uncomfortable knowing it. They may be aware I am staying over at his house or going away with him, but they can still imagine their mother is sleeping on the sofa.

One way of measuring what your children can handle: How often do they call your cell phone? If they overdo the calls, you need to talk with them when you return home. It's not just a purposeful interruption of your intimate moments, but a demand to keep your attention. Speak to them about what they are feeling, then gently inform them that your having a life independent of theirs does not make you love them any less. You are entitled, as they are, to have uninterrupted time with a friend. They wouldn't like you showing up at a friend's sleepover party. You deserve the same liberty.

It helps to be discreet with your teenagers by not flaunting your intimacy with a man in front of them. Remember, they are teenagers, they are chomping at the bit to catch you making a mistake, and as Noble says, "to throw it back in your face when they want to."

When Judith's daughter was fourteen, in preparation for her dating they discussed kissing and sex. As Judith tried to set guidelines, her daughter turned the tables on her mom: "But you're dating four guys!"

"'Yes,' I told her, 'but I'm not doing anything with them.' I'm very cognizant of her seeing me come home at a reasonable hour. I'm not staying out. The men aren't staying over. The reason, I tell her, that I'm dating all these guys is that I haven't found one guy. This is not my preference. We talk openly about it but I worry that she sees me as too loose." If any of the guys were the "right one," Judith adds, the others would be gone.

In Christine's case, her eldest teenage daughter had been seeing a boy for a few months. Christine wondered how she would tell her daughter not to engage in sex and at the same time protect her in case she did. It's like telling your underaged kids not to drink while promising that if they ever do, you will ungrudgingly pick them up. Being parents, we contradict ourselves intentionally because we love and worry about our kids.

Christine told her daughter, "I don't know what you've talked about with your boyfriend, but at sixteen you are not emotionally ready to have sex. However, if you're thinking about ever doing anything, let me set you up with a doctor's appointment."

"You can't stop them," Christine says.

That's true. Your children, just like you as a teenager, will do what they want to do anyway. But they will always look to you as a role model and be attentive, even when you don't think they are, to your actions. Furthermore, you have a valuable opportunity to turn your actions into positive lessons. If they see you date a lot of men, let them understand that your standards are high and you won't settle for just anyone. If they are aware you are sleeping with a man, let them know you reserve this act of intimacy for a serious relationship. If you stay out late with no apparent curfew or go on vacation with a man, let them know they have this to look forward to when they become adults. In time, your children will come around and appreciate that as an adult you're entitled to a different set of rules.

Ryan, now a college freshman, recognizes that his mom should be allowed to do what she wants to because she is thirty years older than he. Sixteen-year-old Lilly agrees: "I think dating someone when you are in your forties is different from dating someone in your teens."

My son, who's observed his mother as a single woman for most of his life, has figured out that I probably hold back from doing things for fear he'll call me on them.

"I feel that there are things you don't do because I'll give you a hard time or do it, too," Noah tells me. He's right. I permitted myself more freedom when he was seven because he didn't understand the meaning of, say, my going away for a weekend with some guy. Today, he does. And although I know he is okay with my doing it, I'm not ready to sanction his doing it with his girlfriend.

There is a distinct difference between your dating as a grown woman and your children dating as teens. You don't need to make excuses for yourself, but to make your life easier and less tense with your children, you should set proper guidelines for them without blatantly violating all of them yourself. Sometimes restricting your own behavior, at least your public behavior, will guarantee you a little more peace in the tumultuous teenage years.

Besides, you're a mother: You're used to always giving in.

❧

CHAPTER SEVEN

Your Kids' Relationship with HIM

All I remember about an artist I dated three times is our last date. He took me to a shady rundown bar for crabs and then to an equally sleazy carnival, where we got stuck on the top of a Ferris wheel. Talk about missed opportunities. Noah, on the other hand, remembers him for his gift of a football-player teddy bear, the yield of a victorious ring toss.

Too bad I wasn't interested in dating the artist a fourth time; he had figured out how to communicate with my seven-year-old son.

Let's face it. If a guy doesn't treat your kids right, he won't last long in a relationship with you. Men, whether or not they are fathers, know this. A man who shows genuine interest in your kids' activities while simultaneously catering to Mom, earns points all the way around. But if he doesn't come by this naturally, he will need directions. And since we all know how men feel about directions, it will be up to you to lead the way.

Play *with* but Don't Play the Kids

Your date may be unsure about how to act with your children. Should he be avuncular and very friendly, or should he remain respectfully distant? You're the guide here since you know your children and which personality they will respond to. Either way, your children need to sense he's sincerely interested in them. Urge your date to treat your children the same way you expect to be treated—with respect. Sandra, who has introduced dozens of men to her children, agrees: "I feel that there needs to be a respectful relationship between them. They don't have to like each other, but it would be nice if they did."

A date must also earn your children's trust. This will only happen if your kids are convinced of two things: first, that you are happy, and second, that this man is genuinely trying to get to know them.

Being attentive to your kids does not mean, in the children's words, "playing" them. They will sense whether the guy is being nice to them just to get to you. It's how he inquires about school or your daughter's art project that your kids will pick up on. If he's patronizing or phony—he's distracted before they answer his questions or he shuts down when you leave the room—your kids will dislike him intensely. If he's thoughtful and curious—he devotes his entire attention to your children—they will like him immediately.

Listen to eighteen-year-old David: "Do *not* play the kids!" Kids, he says, can detect a disingenuous man who only shows an interest in them as a way of getting to Mom.

Equally frank, Molly also hates "people who are fake and would try to play me. Honestly, I'm a big part of my mom's life, and if you want to be one, too, you shouldn't BS me."

You may view a man as trying his utmost to communicate with your children, while they see him as uninterested. Remember, your own perception may be distorted by the combination of emotions you're experiencing in this relationship.

You can't ignore the reality that all of your children—even ambivalent ones, as my son appeared to be as a teenager—will have a relationship with your date outside the one you are experiencing. Noah believes the men I have dated thought they needed to please him. "I always felt they were a little uncomfortable around me and had to get my permission before they did anything."

Since Noah has always seemed more anxious for me to leave with a date so he could snag the remote and take up the entire sofa, I was shocked to learn how, in his own subtle way, he has psyched out my dates.

"If I were to date a single mother, winning over her children would be the biggest feat," my son informs me. "I think a man dating a single mother has to win over the kids."

I suddenly have empathy for the guys I date.

And it's not just my kid. Ryan says that when his mother's long-term boyfriend tried to "buddy up" to him he wanted no part of it. Ryan also delighted in knowing that "he had to get through me to get to my mom. That's what the man feels."

Brian understands both of these perspectives. As a child, he deliberately resisted his mother's dating. Now, as a grown man, he's the guy who dates single moms. His own experiences have made him particularly sensitive to the role of the children: "As in all things, you treat the kids the way you want to be treated." If you're lucky, you will meet a man like Brian who gets it, even without your directions.

Take Max, a fifty-five-year-old father of two adult children about to remarry a mother of three. Max recognizes he has to treat his girlfriend's children like "ordinary people. I have to win them over. I have to recognize they have their own wants and needs. You can't segregate them from their mother."

That's right. Kids are part of the whole package. If your boyfriend can't see this, explain to him the concept of "packages" in a way he'll understand. Beer comes in a six-pack, his new car included undercoating (whatever that is), his tuxedo rental included a cummerbund and tie, and you came with your kids. Not only are your children part of the package, but they never asked for this relationship. Respect them for that. As difficult as they might act—at least in the beginning of your new relationship— insist that your boyfriend treat them with the same deference he shows to you.

He could take a hint from Molly. She says she is not looking for "a friend" in her mom's dates: "But I definitely want a friendly relationship with him. It's also so, so important that he treat me the same way regardless of whether my mom is there."

Help your date to see this. He could irreparably damage a relationship with your children if he acts interested in them while only in your presence. You are the one vested here. If a man fails to win over your kids, it will be nearly impossible for you to handle the roles of both mother and lover. You will be pulled like taffy, becoming weaker and weaker, to the point of tearing apart.

Encourage your date to relax around your kids—really, only a few will bite—and to ask questions that reveal a genuine curiosity about their lives, such as "How's your swim team doing?" Or "What are your plans for the summer?" Gifts, like the teddy bear for Noah, help soften a moment but will have no lasting effect if they aren't succeeded by a continued enthusiasm about the child's activities.

"Oh, he can definitely bring me gifts, but that doesn't necessarily mean I'll like him," Molly says. "Taking an interest in me is important; I think he should want to know about me and who I am. Coming to see my activities or asking me questions is a good way to do that. My mom's last boyfriend asked me to sing for him one time when he was over at the house. That was really nice."

Bonding Isn't Only
Found at the Hardware Store

The sort of activities you plan will help facilitate your boyfriend's developing a relationship with your children. After all, you know their likes and dislikes and can steer him in the right direction.

Lazaroff says that when an activity is completed—the first being something short and sweet like a trip for ice cream—and the boyfriend leaves, "debrief" your kids: "Tell them they can be honest and you know how hard this is for them. Take it one step at a time. The next activity could be board games or athletics or a concert, depending on the age of the kids. But all along, after each outing you should check with the kids and also with the boyfriend to see how he feels, too."

This is key. This isn't just about your kids. It's about your boyfriend, too. It's necessary for your relationship that they *all* get along. So after your date spends time with your kids, ask him if he thought it went okay. A guy may bond more with one child than with another. Brainstorm ways he can gently, and slowly, connect with the more reticent one.

In Christine's case, her youngest daughter was fearful that with Dad remarried and Mom dating, she would be abandoned. This is a natural concern for many kids. Invite those kids to spend time with you and your new boyfriend: Have dinner, pop popcorn, and watch a movie together. Better yet, have your boyfriend extend the invitation. Even if children reject the offer the first few times, by repeatedly including them you will eventually chip away at their worries.

Abandonment isn't the only thing that can worry kids. They may be very concerned about Mom. Julie's overprotective eldest daughter feared that her mom would enter into another dismal relationship like the one she had had with Brett. Consequently, she was reluctant to accept another man in her mom's life. Paul recognized this and decided to give Julie's daughter time to come around. He chose to stay in the background, allowing the relationship between mother and daughter to flourish, and slowly became involved as the daughter began to warm up to him.

"It may take a year to do this the slow and right way," Lazaroff says.

If a child remains distant from your boyfriend, let it go. There will be more natural opportunities in the future for them to connect. You might create a time when your date helps your son with a project. You might be "rescued" by your boyfriend when you and the kids are hampered by a flat tire. You might find your child and your date connecting over a close and exciting basketball game on television. Maybe they'll share a mutual disgust over your always telling them to keep the lid down. Maybe they both hate peas.

If it feels comfortable and natural enough for you to plan organized activities, then definitely go for it. Organized activities have several advantages. Everyone tends to drop his guard, which can be very revealing of someone's personality (Is your boyfriend frustrated with your son for repeatedly hitting the alley with the bowling ball?). It gives you a common experience which creates history ("Remember the time we got caught in the rain on a bike ride?"). And it takes pressure off of everyone as it allows you to focus on the activity itself (Your child may not talk but he loves showing how well he can hit a ball).

Choose activities at which you stink. If you are bad at bowling then go bowling. It will bond your kids and date at your expense.

Julie scheduled a family dinner night every Wednesday and Thursday and would invite Paul over to spend part of the evening with her children: "The kids felt at home in their own environment and were able to be themselves. It also gave them a chance to let him know who they were, as their confidence was always bolstered by the fact that they were all together."

There's safety in numbers, for your kids, at least. But give the guy some credit in these situations. It's not easy being the outsider. Help him succeed by including him in things he does well: sledding, ice skating, school projects, visits to the library, or trips to the arcade. He deserves the same respect from your kids that you expect him to show them. If they are acting ambivalent and then watch your boyfriend do a triple deke on hockey skates, they will find themselves suddenly admiring him. Remind your kids how tough it is for them to be "left out" at school, and ask them to appreciate how this guy feels being an outsider when he's with all of them.

Sandra has always tried to include her serious dates in activities with her kids, often encouraging a guy to play tennis with her son or basketball in the driveway with both kids. Basketball, by the way, is a great way to bond. You don't have to be good at it to have fun. You only need to occasionally aim at the basket. Just remind your date that he's playing against kids and not his college fraternity brothers. His manhood is not at stake here.

Sandra also sets up easy activities with her date and her children that are not necessarily planned, such as preparing dinner or watching a movie or television program at home. She takes advantage of these situations to act as the proverbial fly on the wall and observe their interaction. That's a wonderful benefit to including your boyfriend in casual activities with your kids. It may even be the first time you observe him with his attention focused on others, not just on you. It can be very revealing.

Molly, too, prefers meeting her mother's dates in casual settings, like sporting events or getting ice cream: "You don't want to meet your mom's boyfriend for the first time at some stuffy restaurant where you're just as worried about your manners. And having an activity to do is always good. Its kind of like a first date . . . it's just easier to be playing miniature golf than to be staring at someone across a dinner table."

Getting your date to know your kids takes time. As anxious as you are to create the Brady Bunch, you must allow your children to process the situation and to adjust. In the end, the result will be a much stronger relationship all the way around. Diane's boyfriend, Bill, who has no kids of his own, says he understood that in the beginning he couldn't throw himself at her sons, nor could he overreact: "You do things you'd do in everyday life. They'll either reject you or accept you, but you have to show them who you are."

While you are choosing activities that you know your kids like and that will help them connect with your boyfriend, keep in mind that your boyfriend should be prepared to put his own likes and dislikes aside during this period. If he won't, then you better rethink this relationship. If a guy can't be unselfish during your courting, he probably won't improve when you are married.

Now that Brian has dated a single mother, he recognizes how tough the children can make his role as the mother's boyfriend. He has found it difficult getting his girlfriend's son, a college freshman, to warm up to him. He has tried to find common ground, such as trips to a museum and talks about college—he graduated from the same one: "It will happen the way it's supposed to happen. Kids have to come around in their own way."

You're the Disciplinarian Here, and That's Final, Young Man

If your children are young and misbehaving (What?! Not my kids!) make sure your date knows it's not his place to mete out discipline. It's yours. And you should not be reluctant to punish your child if he is acting out in front of your date. You wouldn't tolerate his hitting his younger sister if you were alone. An added benefit? You'll have an opportunity to observe your date's reaction.

A man should know better in these situations than to discipline your children—he's neither their father nor their stepfather—but how he reacts will be a revelation to you. If he
corrects you in front of your kids and demands to take charge of
the punishment, he's outta there faster than a Barry Bond homer.

A perfect guy will not yell at them, nor roll his eyes, but will
cleverly distract them by suggesting they play a game together or
by getting them involved in another activity. If your relationship
develops long-term, and possibly into marriage, this man will be
more vested in your kids and will naturally progress into occasionally disciplining them—if that is what you want.

Molly says she's happy she's past the age when her mother's
boyfriend would try to either discipline her "or take my father's
place": "And I'm glad about that because I think that's a big mistake boyfriends can make. He should treat me the way he would
treat his niece."

Try as He Might, He Just Can't Win

Sometimes, especially during the earlier stages of a serious relationship, as much as the man defers to your kids, the children
still will not like him. Before you consider breaking up with him,
make an honest assessment of the situation.

As Sandra says, "Are the kids just being protective and unreasonable? Or are they seeing something I am not? If the guy
doesn't get along with my kids, I would have to see if he has issues that are unreasonable. Does he want too much attention at
the cost of my kids? Is he a big baby?"

Ooh. Don't you just hate dating men who increase your brood
by one?

Lazaroff tells her single moms that if the kids don't like the
guy "and you don't want to break up, then you may have to do a

lot of work with the kids and go very, very slowly so they know you are hearing them. You need to explain that you like this man very much and that you will respect their feelings, but that you won't end the relationship."

An announcement like this may help your kids become more responsive to the man's efforts to communicate with them. If they are backed into a corner—Mom is serious and this guy isn't going anywhere—they will more often than not gradually let him into their lives. Be patient. If he is a good guy, it will happen.

If you have had a bad relationship in the past, your kids will go even more slowly. After my second marriage, my kids were cautious about accepting the men who entered my life.

If you've had a bad prior relationship, emphasize the differences in your new boyfriend when discussing him with the kids.

Julie's kids reacted similarly after her relationship ended with Brett. She had never realized how much they disliked him: "They stated that they liked him, but there was always this sense that they wanted to maintain their distance. When I began to date Paul, they felt more concerned about whether or not I should be getting involved again so soon; their concern didn't seem to be about him as a person."

If you are coming off a soured relationship, let your new boyfriend understand that your kids' distance is a result of caution. It isn't personal. Although it may take more effort for him to reach your children, when he does the connection will be strong. Kids will ultimately remove the roadblocks they've set up if they sense a man is genuine.

David viewed his mom's first serious boyfriend as someone who was "more interested in my mom, and 'Oh, you have kids. Okay, I guess I'll be nice to them.'" He saw his mom's second boyfriend, whom she eventually married, as someone who said, "'I will be nice to you, and to your kids.'" See how perceptive your kids can be?

Brian knows this all too well. He believes one reason his new girlfriend's children are not opening up to him is that they've have never liked any of the previous boyfriends. Although they like him, they still need time to develop trust in him.

Sex with Mom? Don't Even Think of It

Men generally are less concerned about whether any of the children—his or yours—become aware you're sleeping together. Yet getting caught in a compromising position will damage their relationship with your children and require a long period of healing. Discuss with your boyfriend how important it is not to let the passion take hold in situations that may compromise you and him with your kids. We've already discussed how *your* relationship with your kids suffers if you're caught in an inappropriate situation. But they at least love you, no matter what. Your boyfriend, on the other hand, could suffer a substantial setback with your children, who will be disgusted by seeing him all over Mom.

Once again, Max is a man who understands this. He says that with the single moms he has dated he's always been very careful about sleeping over: "She's the one who has to explain to the child what's going on. Not me."

That's true, but that in no way lets the man off the hook. Your children will view him differently if they catch the two of you in an awkward moment. They may be embarrassed to speak to the guy on a conversational level. It will take a lot of time for the in-cident to pass before their relationship with him normalizes.

Brian still regrets his girlfriend's teenaged daughter's knowing that her mom had had sex: "I felt absolutely awful about it. I wanted to talk to her: 'You didn't need to hear it. It will never happen again.' I had a hard time not saying anything, but her mother thought it wasn't my place."

Forty-eight-year-old Patrick felt he needed to be honest with his daughters, and so he told them that his girlfriend had slept over: "I was protective of them, but I wasn't going to hide anything from them." Yet while he was telling his kids he was having sex, his girlfriend was telling her kids she wasn't. One day, Patrick's daughters inadvertently let it slip in front of his girlfriend's kids. If you are uncomfortable with your children knowing you are having sex with a man, then insist he respect your feelings and not divulge such news to his own children.

A guy who doesn't understand your desire to keep sex quiet, who insists it's not a big deal if your kids find out, frankly isn't worth staying with. He's correct in saying you are both grown-ups and, as such, entitled to a sexual relationship, but he's wrong if he fails to validate your concerns. If you can't predict with certainty how your kids will feel about knowing you are sleeping with a guy, then don't go there. It isn't worth the repercussions.

He Doesn't Need Kids to Like Yours

Remember the ad I responded to that introduced me to my second husband? It talked about "his, mine, and ours." I naively assumed that a man who was already a father would be a great father to my kids. Conversely, I assumed a man who has never raised kids wouldn't have a clue about how to treat my children. I was wrong. There's no standard rule here.

Sure, being a parent teaches you, as Elise says, "to learn to live outside yourself," but just because a man has never had children doesn't automatically translate into his being a poor stepfather.

A widower I dated after my divorce had never had children, but he had a wonderful relationship with his two nephews and was able to relate to all of my children's issues. In fact, he sometimes had more patience with my kids than I did.

Bill had no children of his own when he married Diane, yet her two boys have affected his relationship with her in many wonderful ways: "There have been days we have issues with the kids. But I've never changed my mind. I knew when I married her there would be tough bridges to cross. But it has been wonderful in a lot of ways. The way I see her raise them gives me a lot of respect for her. It makes me fall in love all over again. Men shouldn't shy away from a relationship just because there are children."

> *A man who's never had kids might act more as an uncle or a family friend to your children than as a father. That might satisfy all parties, especially if your kids are close to their dad.*

He laughs, adding, "Even though at times it makes me want to pull my hair out." Spoken like a parent.

Max, who has two grown kids, accepted his girlfriend's three children as the "total package. I let the children come first. If you are going to go out with someone who has kids, that's her life. Children have to come first. It won't work otherwise. A mother with children . . . that's how it has to be."

The positive news here is that most men will be unfazed by your having children when they first begin dating you. Your being a mother won't be a deterrent. However, as time goes on and a man becomes more serious about you, your children and their relationship with him will matter a great deal.

Patrick admits he had his doubts when he was about to marry his girlfriend because her two sons were giving him a difficult time. But to his credit, he figured he could handle the situation: "I grew up in a stepfamily. When I was ten years old I moved in with four new brothers and four new sisters."

He stuck it out, married his girlfriend, and became a stepfather to two young boys, whom, now teenagers, he adores.

Like Bill, Brian has never raised children but he has a great deal of respect for the relationship his girlfriend's kids have with their mother: "They are the most important things in her life. I think if her kids had some trepidation it would be different. I'm okay with this. Because of my own mom's experience as a single mom, I know where some of this comes from."

Paternal Potential

As discussed earlier, if you set out looking for a man solely to find a father for your kids, you will miss out on satisfying your own needs. Don't sell yourself short. If you go into a shoe store narrow-mindedly looking for a pair of black pumps, you're going to miss the snappy red sandals on the opposite shelf.

In fact, you will serve yourself better if you look for a man you can love and then help him to become a father to your children. Your maternal side will automatically root out the guys you couldn't possibly fall for, such as the man who cringes every time someone's kid cries out at the local pancake house.

Judith worries so much about her special-needs son that she places "a good father" on her short list of priorities in looking for men to date: "I absolutely pick and chose. One guy complained about airplanes' allowing infants on board because they cry. You are not suited for my life, I thought. You will be nice to go to the movies with but not for the long haul." She admits that the guys who have done well are the ones who immediately attach to her son.

Like many children, her son desperately wants a dad. Children want one to round out the family so it feels more normal and so they don't have to go alone to the father–daughter dances or the father–son cookouts. When kids are just beginning to get to know someone you are dating, they are drawn in by physical and materialistic things, such as the man's athletic ability or his cool sailboat. In time, if he becomes a potential stepdad, they'll expect him to act paternal.

How does he show this? If the two of you have plans to go to dinner and your child has a fever, your boyfriend will suggest you stay home and rent a movie (extra points if it's *Finding Nemo* or *American Pie*). An evening like this will go a long way toward strengthening his relationship with your child—not to mention with you when you witness this gentle, loving side.

While a date has to be gracious and civil to your children, he doesn't have to wash the bloody knee of your son when he falls off his skateboard. A possible dad does. A date can say hello when he walks in, while a potential father can kiss or hug, showing some sort of physical affection to your child. Even a teenaged boy appreciates a pat on the back or an embracing handshake.

When you look at a date as a prospective stepfather, you must take everything about the guy into consideration: How does he address your kids? Is he warm and caring? Is he supportive of your difficult role as a single mother? Is he patient with your kids and sensitive to their difficulty in having only one parent at home? Is he willing to change plans so you can include the kids? Your kids will be cognizant of this and will appreciate that he is really trying.

Breaking Up

When you broke up with your boyfriend in high school, the news had little effect on your family. Now as a mother, when you break up with a boyfriend it will have an impact on your children—either positively or adversely. It's very tempting to let your decision to stay or leave be affected significantly by what your children think of him. I know this is difficult, but you need to somehow segregate yourself and your relationship with him from everyone else. If breaking up is in order, because *you* are unhappy, then go through with it.

Your kids know when Mom is miserable. A year into my second marriage, as good a front as I thought I was maintaining, Debra broke my heart one afternoon when she said, "Mom, you're never happy anymore. You're not yourself."

Once you decide to break up, tell him before you tell your kids. You need to make the decision independently of whether or not the kids like him.

So even if you've put on a smiling face, your kids will see right through you. My kids were ten and fourteen when I told them I was ending my second marriage. I was as afraid to tell them that news as I was when I told them I was remarrying. Both times, I was altering their lives. Recently, I learned what Noah had thought: "All those emotional attachments I felt toward him changed the minute you picked me up at school and told me. My feelings instantly changed. I remember that day vividly. If you drive me down that street I can see the point at which you told me."

How does he feel about the men I've dated since? "I've never been emotionally attached to any of those guys. I'll become emotionally attached when there's a man who has made my mother happy."

It always comes back to your happiness. "What makes us happy is what makes my mom happy," David says.

Don't be afraid to end a regrettable relationship because you fear telling your kids. They need to hear the truth. Tell them, "It didn't work out because we have such different ideas in raising kids" or "Because I thought I was in love, I missed our differences" or "He wasn't for me. I didn't realize we were not a match."

Then reassure them: "I've learned so much from this relation-ship and will approach future ones with intelligence and aware-ness. I'm blessed to have had the courage to enter a relationship and the strength to end it when I realized it wasn't right. I still believe in love."

There's no shame in ending a relationship that has not worked out. The only shame is staying in one that you shouldn't.

You have to level with your children about why you broke up, short of explaining something too adult, like he slept with his sec-retary. Tell your kids, "I wanted so much for things to work out with Joe and me because he really took an interest in you and I know it was fun playing tennis with him. But for very adult and personal reasons, it did not work out between us. He and I had dif-ficulties that would have grown over time and would have been very destructive to us as a family. I'm confident that when you get older you will appreciate that I've made the only decision I could."

Sometimes this even means ending a relationship with a man your kids have liked. There may have been a strong bond, one that it might cause you some distress and pain in severing. You have to trust your instincts here. If he is not right for *you*, you've made the right decision in ending it. If your kids have formed an attachment to a guy, you may want to let your kids see him a bit longer. Don't overdo this, and only permit it if he was a really de-cent man whom you just didn't love. Let it fizzle out gradually—no dramatic good-byes. It will. Your kids will get older and more involved with their friends. They'll have less time to go to a bar-becue with your former boyfriend.

Your kids have you. That's really what matters. In time, they'll find someone else with a cool sailboat.

CHAPTER EIGHT

It's Getting Serious

I dreaded the night I told my parents that Charlie and I were getting married. I knew the differences in our religion, age, and experience (my father still couldn't cotton to a worldly ex-Marine loving his innocent little girl) would not be well received.

We invited my parents to my apartment, cooked their favorite (crab imperial), chilled two bottles of wine, and filled the room with Frank Sinatra—a concession on our part.

"I'll take care of it, El," Charlie reassured me as he put the casserole in the oven. "We'll have a drink, a couple hors d'oeuvres, and then sit down for dinner. Afterward we'll go sit in the living room and I'll tell them."

I was delighted to wimp out of this.

As music that sounded foreign in my home intermingled with cooking aromas, I nervously opened the door to my folks. Before I gave them an opportunity to take off their coats, sit down, and dull their senses with the wine Charlie was pouring, I simply blurted out, "We're getting married."

Then I darted into the bathroom to throw up and left poor Charlie out there to pick up the pieces. I never considered that twenty years later I'd face a similar experience.

Never say never.

✳ ✳ ✳

As terrifying as it was to tell my parents I was marrying Charlie— a man they eventually grew to love as deeply as a son—it paled in comparison to the time I told my kids I was engaged to my second husband.

I made the mistake most single moms do. I thought that as I was rolling along in this relationship, becoming more and more serious, my kids were right there with me. Of course they weren't. Most of the three months I had spent with him were without kids—his or mine. The children weren't there in our private moments or when we talked on the phone hours after they had gone to sleep. What felt like an intensely long time to us felt like a skip and a jump to them. They were caught totally unprepared.

With my fiancé in attendance, I broke the news to my children without much more nuance than I had used to inform my parents eighteen years earlier. Noah, only seven, acted appropriately macho and matter-of-fact. Twelve-year-old Debra, stunned and upset and presenting me with a ton of questions—When was it going to happen? Would we live with his kids? Would we still go to Cape May?—ran up to her room. Against my better judgment, I allowed my fiancé to speak to her alone, to explain his love for her mother, as if that would make it all right. Debra, who still needed time to process the news, remained silent. What was I thinking? She was entitled to be alone with her thoughts and then to be alone with me. I should have insisted he wait days, possibly longer, before talking to her by himself.

But then, I had no idea what I was doing.

With the benefit of retrospection, I now know I should have given my kids time to get used to the possibility that Mom would remarry. They had no father from whom to seek comfort, and Mom was pretty useless since she was in love.

As happy as you are with this man with whom you have become serious—so much that you are now contemplating marriage or cohabitation—don't mistake your child's ambivalence so far for expectation and acceptance. Your children probably have been putting up with your dating, not dreaming it could evolve into this. Not only do you need to give them time to process this new development, but you need to validate their concerns, as silly as they might seem—How will we all fit at the kitchen table? Whose TV will go in the family room? Whose dishes will we use? You should let them come around gradually, despite your impatience to move on in this relationship.

Throughout your dating, let your children know if you are becoming serious about someone. All kids, even ones encased in headphones or perpetually hanging out at a friend's home, want to know when Mom's dating starts to turn serious.

Now, at eighteen, David says he was grateful his mom kept him informed. Several years ago, when she told him she was contemplating marriage to a man he disliked, he told her, "I don't know if you'll be happy." His concern left enough doubt in his mother's mind so that she ended the relationship.

A few years later she met a different man, one who was solicitous about her and her kids. When she told her son it was getting serious, David says, "I told her marrying him would make me happy and her, too." In fact, she married the second man, much to her son's delight. In both instances, David's mom had kept her son informed, giving him an opportunity to express his opinion.

As a dating single mother you are placed in the unique position of being the person everyone wants to make happy, while all you really want is for everyone else to be happy. If you choose a man who tries to satisfy your needs and wishes and consequently makes you content, I guarantee your kids will follow.

Among your desires is finding a guy who also happens to be good to your kids. You've been a mother long enough to know when you are around someone who just doesn't like them. The guy Judith dated who thinks crying babies should be banned from airplanes? Put him on a slow boat to China. But a man who is trying to get to know your kids and recognizes how important they are to you deserves all the time and patience you can give him.

Plant a Seed

The best way to prepare your kids for the prospect of your having a serious relationship is to develop trust in the very beginning of your dating life. From that first date, say to your kids that although you are just taking the opportunity to meet lots of men, if you ever find yourself in a significant relationship you will tell them.

"Kids fantasize all over the place," Lindblad-Goldberg says. "If you have a really tight relationship with your kids and you don't say that, your kids will feel left out."

Don't take anything for granted, as I did, and assume your kids know exactly how you're feeling toward a guy. Since many children will be in denial or merely oblivious, they will be staggered by having the news sprung on them.

"It needs to be gradual," Lindblad-Goldberg adds. "In a perfect world, if kids had their way, nothing would ever change. No one would ever die. No one would ever divorce. When you get to the single-parent thing, it would stay that way. A single parent has to be sensitive to kids who are being displaced. If they have been Mom's confidants, they feel they are being displaced. If they represent the absent parent, they will be more judgmental, more critical."

Your kids will notice if you are dating several men or only one. My children have always recognized the implication of my dating a guy a couple of times or over several months and, in fact, that affected how close they allowed themselves to get to him. Noah tells me he has always assumed he had to treat a man who I dated for a long time differently from regular dates: "When you were with a guy longer, I thought I had to spend more time even though you weren't going to get married. I felt it was my duty to be nice."

Lindblad-Goldberg says that if a mom dates a number of people, that communicates "that you have a lot of interests, that you like meeting a variety of people. It's fun for you to meet men with a variety of interests. One person is different. The kids don't have fantasies that Mom will marry if she's dating more than one."

And even though your children recognize you are dating one man and the relationship is becoming serious, they are not necessarily anticipating or looking forward to your remarrying. Kids like what becomes familiar to them, even if it's bad. As much as they might miss being in a family with a father, they eventually adjust to being in a single-parent family. Breaking the news to them that you are becoming serious about someone completely unravels their world: Will you marry him? Where will we live? Are we moving? What about my friends? Where will I go to school? Will his kids live with us? Do I have to share a room?

If you think your kids' concerns are silly, wait until you try to blend his mother's oil-on-driftwood landscapes with your Klee lithograph.

As awful as were the consequences they imagined when you first told them you and their father were getting divorced, that news, at least in how it was presented, more than likely didn't involve strangers. In time, in both divorce and death, your children began to adjust to a single-parent household. Now you hit them with information that involves an unfamiliar man, possibly one with children. The future promises changes that your children may find difficult to absorb.

The only way to give the news of your becoming more serious is to, in Barbara Noble's words, "seed" it, kind of like a developing plant. It grows gradually and you can watch it every step of the way.

"Tell them, 'Joe and I are getting closer. We really do have a lot in common. I like him. He's better than the other dates I've had. He's becoming special to me. I realize I spend a lot of time with him.'"

As a relationship starts to become important, it is crucial you expose this man to your children. That means more than a few quick family dinners and a trip to the movies before you drop the bomb: "We're getting married."

Noble says, "As you're getting more relaxed with someone, you can start dropping little hints about so-and-so. At some point you have to tell them. But as you are happier, they will become happier, too. If you're getting more intense with the guy, you need to tell the children before they hear through the grapevine. That's really important."

Doing this doesn't guarantee your child will like the man, but it does improve your relationship with your child. And that's a great start. The more stable your relationship remains between you and your children, the more willing they will be to accept this new addition. If they think he's weird or unfriendly or cheap, hear them. Your children want to believe they can entrust you with their feelings. They want to know you'll at least consider their viewpoint—especially if they must head into the tumultuous experiences of a blended family. At a time their family as they know it has fallen apart, this openness will instill some confidence in them.

Regardless of their age, all children will react strongly to news that your relationship has become serious. Because their personal issues vary according to their age, so will their reaction.

Children under Eight

Because Noah was seven, he had no clue to the significance of Mom's remarrying. When I told him we would probably sell our house and move into a new one, he excitedly imagined a basketball net and larger bedroom. Besides, he was anxious to replace the circus wallpaper in his room with posters of hockey players and cars. His response was fairly typical for a young child.

"Under eight, kids are pretty accepting. It goes a little better," Beatrice Lazaroff explains. "Young people from birth to eight take life as it is. They don't have the cognitive development to look ahead—to compare and analyze."

Still, even if your children are under eight, you should seed your relationship as it develops more intensely. The passage of time won't be as obvious to them as it will be to an older child, but they should steadily get to know the man and recognize the closeness that exists between the two of you.

By slowly showing affection toward this man, by sprinkling information about him in conversations with your kids, by including him in small family excursions like going for ice cream on a summer's night, you will teach your children that you and he are developing a connection. It will begin to feel more natural to them.

Diane's kids experienced this. They were both under eight when Bill began sleeping on her sofa. His working in her backyard led to his having meals with them and eventually sleeping in the living room. Unlike older kids, they thought nothing of the implications and were completely matter-of-fact when he ended up in their mother's bed. If her kids had been a couple of years older and more sexually aware, it would have been difficult to explain Mom's sleeping with her boyfriend.

In many ways, introducing a relationship to your children is easiest when they are under eight. Their very innocence makes them more accepting of change and trusting of grown-ups, particularly their mom.

Adolescents

Then they turn into adolescents. Adolescents shook up by hormonal and emotional changes self-evaluate daily. And because many aren't opening up, it's easy to mistake their complacency for approval. Yet these are the kids saddled with the most. They love their father. They know where Mom's serious relationship will lead. They probably have friends who are in blended families, and they hear their side of the story all the time.

Lazaroff says kids around eleven and twelve years old, the age Debra was when I became engaged, have a more difficult time adjusting to the news. When they were younger, they didn't look ahead, "but as the brain develops they put two and two together. This is not just a nice man who comes over to have pizza. Who is this guy with his paws on Mom? By twelve, they figure it out."

It is crucial that these children believe they can trust their mom so they can maintain their own sense of security within the family. Honesty and openness will go a long way toward accomplishing that. Don't make promises to these kids that you can't keep. For example, don't tell them you'll never sell the house or make them change schools. You can't predict your future. Yet you can be certain your kids will hang onto every word you say and will throw them back at you if anything deviates.

To foster this trust early in the relationship, tell your adolescent something like "I don't know where this is headed but I like him very much, more than anyone else I have dated. If it becomes so serious that it could lead to marriage, you'll be the first to know. Any decisions he and I make will include input from our families. We all might have to compromise. There's no point in worrying about this now because it may never happen, and if it does, it may be to your delight. I'll keep you posted every step of the way."

Will your children stop worrying? Probably not. But you have just reassured them that nothing will take them by surprise, and that their opinions will be heard. You also have given them a way to address any concerns with you when they feel ready to open up. Keep asking the questions, not prying or repetitive ones, but honest and thought-provoking ones—such as "Won't it be nice to have a huge Thanksgiving this year?"—that don't necessarily demand an answer.

Teenagers

The years from fifteen to eighteen are ones of significant growth and maturity. Teens are going through their own individualization and separation from the family, and their emotions run the gamut. Even if they appear ambivalent, you must keep them informed of your developing feelings for a man. You don't necessarily need to give details—casual remarks will do. When you think it is becoming serious—and well before you have decided on marriage—let them know: "I think I like this guy a lot. I'm enjoying getting to know him better."

Teens today aren't accustomed to dating the way you did at their age. Because they favor hanging out in groups rather than individual dating, they are even more clueless about your social life. Since they are not rushing into relationships themselves, they may not recognize when you do.

Parenthetically, Lazaroff theorizes that group dating may be an outgrowth of 50 percent of kids coming from divorced families:

"There is a problem of kids in divorced families with intimacy in a relationship. I think they are avoiding dating so they won't get hurt."

You can't assume your teenagers comprehend what you are experiencing by virtue of their age. Rather than guessing about what is on teenagers' minds, talk to them; talk to them throughout your relationship with this man. They neither need nor want to hear the nitty-gritty but they should be well aware of your becoming fonder of someone.

You can ease your teen into this idea by saying something to the effect of "I really seem to have a lot in common with Joe. I haven't felt this comfortable with someone in years. He's becoming a wonderful friend. I'm thinking of dating only him for the time being."

Your teenagers will know what that means.

Compromise Is in Order

For any marriage to work, a man and a woman must be willing to compromise on issues ranging from finances to religion. And that's even before the birth of children further complicates matters. Now as you become serious with a new guy, you take your kids along for the ride. You find yourself compromising with him as well as with your kids. There's no easy way to do this. At the very least, hear your children's concerns and wishes. Then communicate with this man you love and compromise again. Return to your kids with a compromise that in the end will probably never make everyone happy, but you do the best you can.

Fourteen-year-old Jeff's mom originally planned to marry in the middle of the school year, a move that would have uprooted him from school. As anxious as his mom and her fiancé were to marry so they could start living together, they decided to delay their wedding, allowing Jeff to finish out the school year. Jeff still had to change neighborhoods, but he found it easier to adjust to the move over the summer. And his mom still married her boyfriend but postponed the wedding six months.

In this case, everyone compromised. While your relationship is taking hold and afterward, when you live together, all of you will need to continue to compromise. Any successful marriage is built on a meeting of the minds. If you and your kids love the beach and he loves the mountains, you might alternate your vacations each year or find a new place all of you can love. If your kids want to rent *Billy Madison* for the umpteenth time and your boyfriend wants *Shindler's List*, figure out a way to give each time to watch. A compromise can also take the form of a bribe, such as allowing your son to spend the weekend at a friend's if he agrees to go to Sunday dinner with your boyfriend. A relationship can survive compromise—it can't survive one person's controlling it, whether it's you or him or your child.

In fact, your kids might try to exert control by putting up roadblocks, not because they want to see you miserable, but because they are afraid. They might demand you stay home and help with homework or they might refuse to answer the phone when caller ID identifies your boyfriend. If you are marrying an all-around great guy—not only from your perspective but from your kids'—eventually your kids will acquiesce.

Ryan regrets refusing to accept the man his mother fell in love with until it was too late. The man was transferred from the East Coast to California, and Ryan's mother's job and family prevented her from going with him. "It was tough on her," he says repentantly. "I never really allowed myself to get to know him." If Ryan had had more time to adjust to his mom's relationship with this guy, he knows he would have become more accepting. Time. Seems like an easy compromise. But when you are passionately in love with someone and want to be with him day and night, you'll find time to be the hardest thing on which to compromise. Nevertheless, as a single mother, you really have little choice.

As long as you don't rush into marriage or even engagement, as I did, there is time to allow your children to become accustomed to this man's becoming a permanent feature in their life. Although it may mean you don't live together just yet, it doesn't preclude your seeing him frequently, talking about him constantly, and having him appear with you in your kids' presence regularly.

It will become routine, so much so that even your teenagers may begin to accept his staying over or going away with you on vacation.

Dad Remarries

As a single mother you are likely to find yourself handling the fallout with your kids when they learn Dad is remarrying. It may be difficult for you to speak favorably about your ex-spouse and his new wife, especially if she's the reason for your divorce, but you will find yourself with healthier, better-adjusted children if you can pull it off.

Look at your ex-spouse's remarrying positively; you are guilt-free to date, you're moving on, and now he's someone else's project.

Concentrate on not badmouthing your children's father or his new wife in front of them. Save the bashing party for your girlfriends. Be supportive if not downright complimentary of this couple. In the end your kids will respect your judgment since it's not clouded by jealousy or bitterness. You will look great, not only in front of the kids, but in front of the ex-husband who gave you up.

For years my son played hockey with a boy whose mom and dad attended every game and always appeared cordial, warm, and relaxed with each other as we all froze in the bleachers. One day the father showed up with another woman, and I asked the mom who she was. "She's his wife," she told me. I was shocked to discover that this couple had been divorced, because frankly they seemed to have a better relationship than most of the married parents. The credit goes entirely to the mom.

"I do it for the kids," she said. Her efforts to keep up a front were admirable and resulted in her children's growing up extremely well adjusted and comfortable being with either parent. There's no question this is easier said than done, but the rewards are worth the effort.

When Caitlyn's dad remarried, she was furious. Eleven at the time, she was confused and unwilling to give her father's new wife a chance. Her older sister, Lilly, says the news that their father was remarrying came as a shock. He hadn't given them any time to get to know his fiancée and, consequently, they had assumed he was still dating several women. "My dad kept his personal life very private from us," says Lilly. "Prior to meeting his wife, we met only two other women."

Caitlyn admits that the news of her father's remarrying devastated her because she had never given up hope that her parents would reconcile.

When you or your ex-spouse becomes serious about someone again, you will be forced to reiterate to your children that Mom and Dad are not reconciling. Even if you think your kids should be aware of this, in most cases they aren't. You have to be sensitive to their feelings but firm in your own personal commitment to moving on with your life.

Sit your kids down and tell them you understand what they are feeling. Say, "I know you'll never stop wanting Dad and me to get back together. We both wish it had worked out for all of our sakes. But sometimes that just can't happen. I'm sorry you're feeling pain, but this is how it needs to be. I assure you that one day it will make more sense."

As much as they should hear this from both of their parents, often it's left up to you to have this conversation alone. This is all about leveling with your kids, being honest, and validating their pain, all the while recognizing your own needs.

Then when it comes time to tell your children you are remarrying, they will be more resigned. Jeff says that when his mom told him she was remarrying, it was easier to accept because his father had done so earlier: "It wasn't as though one of them was trying to get back together and the other was remarried. They both were."

Introducing All the Kids: And You Thought Détente Was Tough

Ranking up there with the gut-wrenching announcement that you are about to remarry is the day you arrange for both sets of kids to meet. This can occur even before you are serious and contemplating marriage. It can happen when there is a man with whom you expect a long-term relationship and, logistically, want the children to meet so you can share common events like holidays or vacations.

My son still remembers the first time he met a child of a man I was dating. Noah was seven at the time and the man's child was five. The four of us went to a Phillies game, and before long Noah found the guy's son annoying.

The boy demanded everything from his dad, who happily delivered. He asked for pizza. His dad bought it. After two bites, he asked for cotton candy. His dad flagged down the vendor. After a pull of that, he stuck it under his seat and demanded ice cream. His father went out to buy that. The game was a succession of get-me's and I-want's. While Noah fixated on the boy's asking and receiving things he didn't even eat, I was done in when the father wouldn't buy himself a *kosher* hotdog, figuring there were cheaper ones in the stadium. There weren't. When we got back into his car to head home, I turned to look at Noah sitting in the backseat next to my date's son. The not-too-subtle roll of Noah's eyes told me that my first experience introducing children was a failure.

First of all, I was not seriously involved with this man, nor did I think I ever would be. Second, going to a baseball game for an initial meeting was way too long an encounter for the kids. Meeting for pizza probably would have made more sense. Third, I should have met his kid by myself first, do sort of a recognizance mission, and be able to come back and warn my son. At the very least, maybe his son would have been slightly more comfortable with me if it hadn't been our first meeting, and he wouldn't have sought his dad's attention so desperately.

I learned my lesson. After that experience, I only introduced my kids to a man's children when the relationship was developing long-term. More often than not, these experiences were positive ones. My kids enjoyed getting together with the widower I dated who had two sons. His kids and mine had similar interests— hockey and snowboarding—so they immediately found a common ground, which took the pressure off us. I had already met his kids several times and had talked about my kids to them before we ever brought all of them together.

In another case, a man I dated for a year had one daughter the same age as Debra. The two girls bonded beautifully over their mutual recognition that their parents—he and I—were hopelessly dorky.

Noble notes, "The kids will be curious to meet the other kids. So have something where you bring them all together or meet somewhere. He's had a relationship with your kids. You've had somewhat of a relationship with his kids. You invite each other to family functions."

One creative and fairly successful way of introducing kids was organized by Melanie, who, as much as she loved her new boyfriend's getting to know her kids, had been in no rush to meet his. He had three, ranging in age from eleven to sixteen.

"I felt fine with his meeting my kids," she says. "But he had protected his kids from me for six months. Now he asked me to meet them. The little one was close to his mom and had not wanted to meet me. This puts a different spin on things. I think because he had held back on my meeting his kids, that put even more weight on it."

Melanie arranged for all the kids to meet at a mall. The two families gathered at a certain time, introduced themselves, and then separated for a while. They planned to come together later over lunch. Combining the kids is always somewhat awkward, but her way allowed the kids to take notice of each other and then take some time to process what they had seen before all sitting down for lunch. Try this, rather than inviting his kids to your home. It's neutral territory, and it doesn't feel so confining to any of the kids.

If she could have handled it differently, Melanie would have arranged to meet his kids first without hers being present. But she was unnerved by the significance placed on meeting the kids: "I got a little nauseated when he asked me to meet them. What if his kids didn't like me? They could make his life miserable."

Introducing your kids may not always go smoothly. When Roseanne realized she had fallen in love with Robert, she made arrangements for all the kids to meet over dinner. But her oldest son, who was ten at the time, refused to get out of the car. Dinner was canceled. The next time, when they decided to go to Robert's house, her son wouldn't leave her side.

Roseanne now knows that she rushed things. First, she surprised her children with the news of her relationship with Robert, and then she told them it was serious. Her sons' discovery that Robert had two daughters further complicated the situation. Her kids had no time to adjust to these developments.

Don't push the blended family. It needs to be gradual and non-threatening. Sometimes children just need to mature. Roseanne's son and Robert's eldest daughter clashed for years over such hot-button issues as taking too long in the bathroom and blasting the stereo while the other one was sleeping. But when the two turned sixteen and realized they needed to share a car, they bonded.

Although two sets of kids definitely complicate a serious relationship, that doesn't mean they are a detriment. They add another dimension. You are likely to find yourself adoring his children and he will yours. Before you commit to a man with children, it is critical you spend time with him in their presence.

In a perfect world, neither yours nor his will be manipulative and everyone will get along great. But first, the two of you have to strike a delicate balance, making each other a priority while remaining loving and considerate of your kids.

You both need to recognize how you react to your own kids. If he caters to his daughter at your expense, then think long and hard about whether this is a man you want to live with. On the other hand, if he recognizes his daughter's manipulation and refuses to give into it, he has great promise as a partner to you. Cass and Phillip both felt they had a realistic understanding of their own children. They understood that each of them had a child who was trying to undermine their relationship. Rather than allow that to happen, the couple cohesively agreed not to relinquish control to the kids.

In Diane's case, as much as she loved Bill, she knew she couldn't marry him unless he loved her kids, too. Bill became close to her sons, an easy adjustment since he had no kids of his own. "I knew he loved me but he also had to love my kids," Diane says.

Although it has taken Roseanne years, she now loves Robert's children.

"At first I felt as if I wanted a lot of kids, so I was excited about suddenly having daughters," she says, but the first few months and years of fighting between her older son and Robert's daughter made for a "horrible" family life: "But I learned. You're never going to love someone else's kids the way you do your own. I had to accept he couldn't love my kids the way he did his own."

Kids, We're Getting Married

Assuming you've done everything right—you've been the perfect, caring, completely unstressed single mom; you've dated one lovely man a very long time, all along asking your kids' opinions; and you've found the perfect affordable new house with stables, a pool, and a tennis court in the same school district with enough rooms for each kid to have her or his own bedroom and bathroom—then announcing your marriage should be a piece of cake.

For the rest of us, it may go over like a ton of bricks.

Be prepared for a lot of questions to which you must have answers. Then, when the time comes to tell your kids about your plan to remarry, tell them alone, without your boyfriend present. You're not asking their permission. You're telling them you're doing this, but you want to know how they feel about it.

Telling them alone, you with yours and he with his, allows the kids to voice their concerns. When I told my kids I was remarrying, I should have waited until he left my house, then gathered my two children together to tell them. You would have thought I'd learned from the first time with Charlie. It wouldn't have changed the outcome, but I think it would have put me on clearer footing with my kids, especially my daughter. I set the stage immediately that we were losing the special single-parent family bond by allowing him to be present when I broke such extraordinary news.

"I feel that you need to tell your kids alone and he needs to tell his kids alone. They can express satisfaction. If they cry, why does he need to know that?" says Noble.

Jeff feels differently from most kids in that he wishes he had been told jointly by his mom and her boyfriend, all the kids together: "It would have made it seem as though we all had a say in it. If they were there together, they wouldn't be able to say I don't like that person."

Still, Jeff says, when he learned that his mother was going to marry this man who had been hanging around a lot, he wasn't surprised: "I kind of felt as though it was bound to happen sometime. I wasn't in shock. I didn't say anything when she told me. I just accepted it."

But his eleven-year-old brother reacted with anger and disgust. His mother's remarrying meant moving into the man's house, a change in schools, and a stepsister close to him in age whom he disliked.

"I'm okay with it," Jeff says. "I like it. My brother and the man's daughter don't get along. It's a problem in that way."

When Cass broke the news to her kids, her older child's "jaw dropped and he said, 'Oh my God.'" Her younger son had a conniption and screamed, "No way, I'm not going to be part of a stepfamily. You can't make me live with them. You're going to ruin my life." Cass says she uttered some soothing words and then left him alone to process it.

How can you tell your children such news? Warn them ahead of time rather than going into their room while they're studying or dropping the news in a car (I'm terribly guilty of unloading news on my kids while I hold them captive in the passenger seat. No wonder they now offer to drive). Tell them earlier in the day, "I'd like a few minutes later to talk to you about Joe and answer any questions you might have about where our relationship is headed."

"Are you guys getting married?" you may be asked.

"We have discussed that possibility, but I really want to talk to you and your brother." Here you've introduced the idea but you haven't committed to anything, and you've indicated there will be an opportunity to voice their opinion. Later, when you talk about marriage, your conversation could go like this:

"I've been alone a long time, and once you leave for college, I'll be even more alone. I've been so fortunate to have found Joe. I love him very much and would like to spend the rest of my life with him. He feels the same way."

"Are you guys getting married?"

"Well, we'd like to. In fact, very much. It would mean we would live together and his kids would stay with us when they aren't with their mom. It'll take some adjustment on all of our parts, yours and ours, but it'll make us a very special family. You'll still have me, and my love for you guys is forever, and you'll have Dad, but now you'll also have a stepdad who happens to be very fond of you."

The questions will follow regarding living arrangements, school changes, time and place for the marriage, and whether they can tell their friends. Answer these honestly. If you don't have an answer yet, admit that. Then offer to allow them to be part of those discussions as well. Your boyfriend may need the same guidance from you in approaching his own children.

In Julie's case, her first serious boyfriend after her breakup with Brett told the kids about his marriage proposal in a most considerate fashion. That man, Paul, informed her children—including her recalcitrant eldest daughter—before he even asked Julie. They hadn't grown to love him yet, but they immediately trusted him for respecting them enough to involve them. Later that day, seated at a folding table, graced with a bottle of wine and a vase of roses, and placed on the site where they would build a new home, he proposed. An astonished Julie said yes, then panicked when she realized she now had to tell her kids. She and Paul returned to her house, where, unbeknownst to her, all the kids—his and hers, and both sets of parents—were waiting to celebrate.

Now there's a man worth cloning.

Once your children accept your remarrying, you can't pressure them or expect them to love their future stepfather. This isn't their obligation. He may become your husband and your children's stepfather, but that doesn't necessarily translate into being a "dad" to your kids. Let your kids off the hook. They didn't choose this man as a father, and chances are they already have or had one they adored.

Elise tells her kids, "You only have one father regardless of whatever happens, and no one will ever replace your father. I'll never expect you to view someone else the way you do your dad."

While this is true, it is likely that in time your children will grow fond of their stepdad if they see you happy. As they get older and they witness how he cares for you and how that takes a burden off them, they will feel good about him.

> "When I told my daughter I was remarrying, she was furious. I told her, 'She's not going to try to be your mom. She won't replace your mom. You don't have to like her kids. You'll have your room. You'll still have camp in the summer.' She eventually came out of her room, and I remember thinking it's going to be okay."—Phillip

Playing House Instead

There are times you may find it more appropriate to live with someone rather than rush into marriage. Because adolescent children put demands on any marriage, Lindblad-Goldberg says you may want to consider dating or cohabiting until your kids are grown. Also, it is easier legally and financially to untangle yourself from cohabitation than from a marriage, and certainly if there is any doubt in your mind, try living together first.

I recently attended a party where I met a woman who, after two marriages and subsequent divorces, had renounced future relationships. Then, one day, overly stressed at her high-powered New York City job, she spontaneously took time off to go on a sailing trip. There she met another passenger, a Canadian man who was nine years her junior and had never been married. They felt an immediate attraction, but when the three-week trip was over, they returned to their homes—thirty-five hundred miles apart. Because they missed each other, the woman took a four-week leave of absence from work and went to visit him in his small rural town. They fell in love. But she was dubious about remarrying for a third time, so she agreed to live with him instead. Compromising on a location two hours outside Manhattan, they cohabited for four years. Then, one day, the doubts and concerns having evaporated, she confidently consented to marriage. That was ten years ago. She still glazes over like a newlywed when she talks about her husband.

Living together, of course, is always less complicated to arrange if your kids are grown. It's easier to compromise with your boyfriend on location if you're not anchored by your children's lives. Plus, given a choice, most older children would prefer Mom's holding off on living with a guy until they're out of the house.

My son tells me, "Once I'm out of the house for good, you can live with someone. But I come first. I think it would be weird if someone were living there and I'm at home. But on the other hand, I don't want to leave and think you're alone."

And Molly says she would vehemently disapprove of her mother's living with a guy if she disliked him. "I think if I didn't like the guy, she shouldn't even think of living with him."

First of all, you need to be at ease with the concept of living with a man out of wedlock. Then you need to consider the age of your children. Very young children will be ignorant of the controversy about cohabitation, while adolescents and teenagers may be uncomfortable. This is a very personal issue and must be made based on your own beliefs and in consultation with your children.

Whose Name Goes on the Mailbox?

Although the most difficult part in blending two families when you marry or live with a man are the children, there are many other issues to consider.

In marriage, should you change your last name to his? As an established journalist, I had kept my maiden name during my marriage to Charlie, who was a very secure, self-possessed man. Then, when he died, I hated that my children's last name differed from mine, so I took his last name. When I remarried, I felt my new spouse needed the reassurance, so I changed my name to his. After my divorce, it took me years to extricate myself from his moniker. I'll never change my name again.

But that's me. You will do what feels right to you.

You might feel that changing your name will make your children feel disconnected, especially in a blended family where they are the only people with a different last name. This is a highly personal issue with no right or wrong. When I first kept my maiden name back in the seventies, it was not very commonplace, and a lot of folks automatically assumed Charlie and I weren't married. Today, it is common for young women to keep their maiden names after marriage, so your having a different name from your kids will be less an issue.

> *"I changed my name back to my maiden name after my ex-husband remarried. I didn't want two Mrs. Smiths around. I found it very liberating."*
> *—Christine*

And the name on the mailbox? Skip it. In a blended family there is likely to be more than one surname living under the same roof.

Then there are the family pictures, his and yours. Melanie admits her house is still filled with photographs of her ex-husband because she simply hasn't gotten around to getting rid of them yet. Even Gladys has a few photographs of her children and her ex-husband from family vacations. Yet she acknowledges that when she was dating her one serious lover, she was bothered that he had his wedding picture on display with his and his late wife's wedding rings hanging from the frame: "After we dated eight or nine months, I mentioned it to him, and he finally took it down."

Cass, too, displays family photos that include her ex-spouse, but her fiancé, Phillip, says, "I don't care about her past." She also has no intention of telling Phillip to remove the photos of his late wife when they all live together.

"I can't take those down," says Cass.

As a widow, I still have family pictures of Charlie in the living room and our wedding picture—resurrected after my divorce—on my bedroom bureau. If I plan to remarry or live with someone, I will give the wedding picture to one of my kids, who may choose to put it in his or her room. I would expect some of the family pictures to remain.

Any decision about what pictures will be displayed when you remarry or live together has to be made jointly with your boyfriend. If there are no children involved, it would be unlikely you'd display any pictures of his or your former spouses. Children pose a different problem. These pictures, after all, include their other parent and are memories of good times as a family. Compromise is in order once again. You and your significant other can select photos you can live with—family shots, not wedding pictures. What his or your kids choose to keep in their rooms is up to them.

Perhaps one of the biggest questions when combining families is where you should live. Assuming your homes are close enough so that you can remain in the same general area, consider the possibility that all the kids may be happier on neutral ground. Granted, sometimes there are practical needs. Your house is a perfect size and has no mortgage. He's living in a condo where he is paying an exorbitant monthly fee. If your decision is to share your house, then you will need to make room for his kids so they do not feel they are visitors. It has to be their home, too. Make space on the towel rack for their towels, fill your pantry with foods they like, and involve all the kids in sharing household chores.

Because kids like to think they are getting some benefit out of their parent's new relationship, it's not unusual for parents to bribe them, possibly with a television in their room or a pool table, as a way of sweetening the reality of a blended family. There's nothing wrong with this. If your or his children think they are getting *something* out of the deal, they will be slightly more willing to give. If one child gets the larger bedroom, the other child should be given his own space in the basement to set up his drums. It goes back to compromise.

And what about blending the pets? His cats, your dogs. Will Fido and Fluffy get along? If either of you has an ex-spouse, first try to get him or her to take your pets. That way your kids can still visit their pets. If you have no choice but to combine all the animals, call your veterinarian and get some suggestions for blending the pets.

And speaking of ex-spouses: While having no right to intervene in new relationships, if there are kids involved more than likely they will, especially if they haven't remarried themselves. You and your serious boyfriend must be bonded here, loyal and responsible to each other. Your first obligation lies with this man and not with your former spouse. The ex-spouse can undermine your relationship by digging in through the kids. The guilt your new spouse's kids feel in becoming close to you, for example, is usually an outgrowth of not wanting to be disloyal to their other parent. Before you remarry, the man must understand that his former wife—although his children's mother—does not serve a function in your new life together.

The best you can hope for—and I'm not beneath facilitating this if necessary—is to have that former spouse contently lodged in his or her own new relationship.

✻ ✻ ✻

Don't ever allow the challenges of being in a serious relationship to prevent you from entering one. If you've found a wonderful guy to marry or to live with, take the plunge. If he is a fantastic guy, your children will eventually come to realize that, and all of your lives will be more fulfilled.

Blended relationships don't normally end because of the children but because you or he forgot about each other and allowed the kids to take control. It is difficult not giving in to your children, especially since you feel bad that their home has been disrupted, but it will be impossible for you to maintain a healthy relationship with the man if you both constantly let your kids rule.

If you and your new spouse remain solicitous of each other, not only will your children respect you both in the long run, but they will learn from you how two adults can achieve a strong marriage.

Epilogue

A s you approach or even exit middle age, in case you're won-
dering if it's too late to date I need to introduce you to my
friend Doris's mom.

Dorothy remained single for forty years following the death of
her husband. When she turned eighty-four, but only after years
of prodding from her daughter, she reluctantly agreed to sell her
house and move into a retirement complex. There one Friday
night, while twirling on the social-hall dance floor, she met
eighty-two-year-old Leo. A year later, dressed in pink chiffon
with matching pumps and with her children and grandchildren
in attendance, she married him. Today in their nineties, they
shamelessly act like a couple of newlyweds.

Sure, no single woman wants to wait forty years to meet the
man of her dreams. But Dorothy and Leo's story just goes to show
that you never know where or when you'll find love. It can appear like an unexpected sun shower leaving a rainbow in its
wake. In the meantime, enjoy your kids and your life.

As Judith says, "Don't think about the dating. Fix your relationship with your kids. Take care of your heart, mind, and spirit.
You won't need to look. The men will be all around."

So what's happened to our single moms? Did Sandra ever meet the man of her dreams online? Did Sally's daughter ever come to terms with her mom's dating? Did Julie ever get over Brett and marry someone else? Did Roseanne find happiness with the guy she hid in her closet?

All the single moms you have gotten to know in this book have reached a point of contentment and are engaged in healthier relationships with their children. Although some are still looking for Prince Charming, others have already found him.

Nearly all who sought their own personal happiness as a goal achieved it. Being single, they learned, doesn't equate with being sad, while being married doesn't necessarily equate with happiness.

How right they are.

* * *

After swearing off men following the breakup of a long-term relationship, Cass has since married the widower of her best friend, and the two have combined their families in a new house "with enough bedrooms for everyone to have their own—fresh start, no memories." And the kids are getting along better, finally recognizing that regardless of their contrariness, their parents are married. Now they just fight like typical siblings. Cass says, "Time seems to have helped a lot. Everyone is more used to each other, so they are more willing to make it work."

Meanwhile, her own children's relationship with that former boyfriend, who continued to see them despite the end of his relationship with Cass, gently faded away as they developed feelings toward their new stepfather.

"I still feel like one of the luckiest people in the world," Cass says.

* * *

Melanie's fondness for the man she met in a bar has blossomed into "head-over-heels" love. Her kids have become much more accepting of their mother's relationship: "I'm a better parent because I'm happy. I feel more nourished, more balanced. I don't give them all that I gave them before, but I'm a whole lot happier and I don't get angry. The whole house is a whole lot better."

Melanie's boyfriend hasn't stayed overnight since the morning she forgot her son was taking the SATs and instead—with her kids' approval—she stays at his house two nights a week. She has decided that her boyfriend will not move into her home until her kids are grown and out of the house. "We talk about our level of commitment with each other—but we don't discuss marriage yet. I'm enjoying my two kids."

✳ ✳ ✳

Although Sally no longer feels the need to lie to her daughter about her dating, her daughter continues to act out. A year ago Sally met a man on Match.com who has been patient and loving despite her daughter's anger: "He's very good to me and I'm not going to discourage him." Sally works with a therapist to understand strategies for dealing with her daughter and is making some progress.

"I know I'm better, healthier than a year ago," she says. "It is a long, slow road."

✳ ✳ ✳

Remember that polite, soft-spoken man whom Gladys met at a charity function and who boldly asked to sleep with her on their second date? The two fell in love and continued a wonderful relationship for more than a year before, sadly, he died after a short-term illness. For the following year Gladys chose not to date but now feels ready to resume: "Because that relationship was such a powerful and fulfilling one, it's a double-edged sword. What it means is that I feel that I have a new standard with which to judge people, which is unfair to them. But I want to date again and develop relationships. I think my kids will be much more understanding than they were and more willing to give the guys a break. I think this one relationship probably broke the ice on a lot of fronts."

In the meantime, Gladys has taken on a new job that involves travel, conventions, and meetings and has remained very involved in her charitable causes. It's just a matter of time, in her mind, until she meets someone at these social and business functions.

✳ ✳ ✳

Rachel still cringes when she remembers the night her naked boyfriend—the man she met on the crowded dance floor of a local bar—came face to face with her teenaged son in the upstairs hallway. Only now, she's able to laugh about it. She and Neil married, and he has become a wonderful stepfather to her three sons. He moved into her home so the marriage wouldn't disrupt her children's lives.

And now Rachel actually lets him keep his clothes in the master bedroom—neatly folded and put away, of course.

✳ ✳ ✳

Carol, after years of feeling guilty about all the men who stayed overnight while her son was home, has developed a renewed strong and close relationship with her now adult son—a father himself. Carol's dating has been preempted by her opening a new business, which has been both successful and rewarding: "I must admit that I constantly miss my little boy, who often appears in my thoughts and dreams. He never deserved the lousy deal he got as a child. I did everything backward. Maybe I should have been home with him then and dating now. Perhaps I can be a better grandparent than I was a parent."

✳ ✳ ✳

Roseanne married the man who hid in her closet, and after a couple rocky years of adjusting to a blended family, her kids love their stepdad: "We were lucky. It's still hard but Robert has been very patient about the kids. I can be an emotional wreck, but we always tell each other when we feel we aren't being nice to each other's kids. It hurts but we always manage to let it roll off our backs."

Would she have handled her dating any differently or held off on marriage until her kids were out of the house? "Oh, God, no!" Roseanne states emphatically.

✳ ✳ ✳

That landscaper who worked for Diane is now her husband and the stepfather to her two children. Sometimes she feels guilty that she got a second chance after a dismal first marriage: "I'm very happy. Bill and I are lifemates. It doesn't matter how many wrinkles I get. He'll look at my face and say, 'They're years of experience.' It is possible to have a happy second marriage with kids."

Her one error, she sees, is that because she criticized her ex-husband to Bill with some regularity, today Bill detests him. That makes getting together at functions concerning her children very difficult: "If I had tried to handle all the stuff with my ex-husband myself, Bill wouldn't have such hard feelings."

✳ ✳ ✳

Sandra continues to date scores of men, mostly through the Internet personals. She admits her standards are high, and she refuses to overlook certain characteristics, like looks or intelligence. "Life is too short to settle," she says. In addition to the Internet and dating services, Sandra has begun attending more business-related functions, hoping to network both professionally and socially. Her children are a fulfilling part of her life, and her career has taken off: "The rest of my life is very busy, good busy."

✻ ✻ ✻

Elaine's daughter is now grown and out of the house, so she's lifted her self-imposed ban on dating and is anxious to "seek the meaning of many things, including love, lust, and the like!" Rather than wait for a guy to spot her, she mustered up the courage to ask out a younger coworker. Stay tuned.

✻ ✻ ✻

After several years of dating as a widow when her children were young, Maribeth met a man online and married him. He and his children moved in with her family, but after a year it became obvious it wasn't going to work out and they divorced. She's been dating happily ever since, and her children, now teenagers, are very supportive. She's also developed a newfound respect for washing machines. Oh, and remember the partner of her late husband, Anthony? She never heard from him again.

✻ ✻ ✻

Elise has lost her sex buddy. She was devastated to learn that he had found a girlfriend, which meant the end to their sexual relationship. She's in the market for a new one. In the meantime, she still hasn't put a picture of herself on the Internet, which limits her online dating. However, her dating scores of men has helped her hone her search.

One of her long-term relationships ended when the man met someone at his high school reunion: "I'm just going to go ahead and do things that I enjoy in my life. I made my decision to get out of my marriage and got comfortable living my life alone, but after you've had a romantic involvement you get lonely. There's that renewal: 'I can feel again.' The bad side is that there is a chink in the armor and you're not so willing to be alone again."

She's back online, welcoming any and all fix-ups, and getting involved in singles events and gourmet clubs.

* * *

For a time Julie left Paul to go back with Brett. Fortunately for her, Paul knew she'd be back and waited. That piece of land where he had set up a table, wine, and roses to propose now rests under the house they and the kids have moved into. "I'm doing really well," Julie says. "We've been on fast-forward ever since we've been married, with the kids, Paul's new grandchild, and the house. I think Paul would like more free time. You need to enjoy the journey, too."

Her eldest daughter, who had always been reluctant to accept her mother's dating, has improved. She likes and respects Paul but still wants—and gets—some "mom time": "If anything, my relationship with my kids has gotten better because being with Paul has enabled me to do more things with them."

The irony is that nine years ago, someone wanted to fix her up with the "perfect guy" but she was still in her tumultuous relationship with Brett and turned down the offer. That perfect guy, who thankfully resurfaced years later, was Paul.

✳ ✳ ✳

Christine's daughters have come around to accepting their mother's dating, especially since they are now finding themselves with plans on Saturday nights and can't bear to watch their mother sit home alone. Christine dated one man seriously whom she met through a dating service, but her kids didn't like him: "When push comes to shove, if I have to choose what makes me happy or my child, I'll pick my child. I'm pretty happy. I'm a little bit spiritual, and I do wake up every morning counting my blessings."

✳ ✳ ✳

Judith continues to date, looking at guys as potential long-term partners. Otherwise, in her mind, it's a waste of her time: "I have a career that takes a lot of time. I have a lot of female friends. I'm not dating men because I don't get out. I'm not dating men because I'm lonely. If these guys clearly are not prospective long-term partners, it's a waste. I have money to pay for my own dinner. The dating scene for me is about finding someone who will be a lifelong partner."

She continues to see the man she met on the plane. He lives in New York City, and she lives in Texas. Despite the distance, their relationship has gotten stronger. They visit each other during business trips and talk on the phone all the time. Closer to home she's ended a couple of relationships, including one with a man fifteen years younger who wanted to settle down with her, and she continues to meet men, including one online.

She says, "I was grocery shopping the other day and two men approached me and gave me their cards. I think I have an energy.

I'm not looking for it. You have to detach yourself from the out-come and let things happen." Her children are both doing well, finally adjusting to their mother's dating and feeling confident that they don't have to compete with her dates for her love and attention.

✽ ✽ ✽

And now this brings us to me.

A year after Charlie passed away my friend Susie told me that a guy she knew had seen me at an event and had inquired about me. "That's nice," I thought. "But I'm not ready to meet anyone." A year later our mutual friend, Fran, threw a birthday party for her husband, and Susie pointed across the room toward a good-looking guy in a black turtleneck. "That's the guy who asked about you."

Okay, so now I was ready. But he wasn't available. Over the next ten years—during which I remarried, divorced, and dated many men—I'd occasionally run into him at various functions. When he was interested, I was attached. When I was interested, he was attached. It became very awkward.

Then sadly, two years ago Fran's husband, Mark, a college fra-ternity brother of this man, suffered a heart attack and went into a coma. During the nearly six months until his death, I visited Mark often. He had been a wonderful friend to me and to my children. Call it fate, or coincidence, but it seemed that every time I went to visit Mark, whether it was morning or evening, the guy in the black turtleneck picked the same time to show up.

After weeks of meeting at the hospital, one day he suggested we get together for dinner. We did. That was two years ago. He's a really great guy, smart and sweet. My kids like him. My friends like him. Even my mom approves.

And he doesn't kick my cat.

Acknowledgments

Over the years whenever life handed me challenges, I'd tell family and friends, "They're just more fodder for my book." With the help of some talented and caring people, that fodder has now been turned into these pages. I want to thank my editor, Ingrid Finstuen, who saw me through the writing, and Perseus's Marnie Cochran, Kate Kazeniac, and Erica Lawrence, who saw me through the fun stuff. I am also grateful to my agent, Susan Cohen, who believed in this book, and in me.

But none of this could have been written without the women, men, and children who allowed me to pry into their personal lives in order to create something meaningful for single moms. Although the names of those interviewed have been changed in this book, some have permitted me to thank them publicly. They include Brenda Bazan, Lisa Dekis, Theresa and Joe Froshour, Rachel and David Cantlay, Martha Macartney, Lilly Palmieri, Shelley Miller, Cynthia Gilmartin, Helen Bosley, Vickie Cohen, Robin Cherkin, Robin and Bill Pearson, Barbara and Paul Averill, Robert Prusinowski, Sam Schmader, Julia Kay, Dana Uttal, Catherine Uttal, and Will Dewey.

A huge thank-you goes to the psychologists who gave of their professional time and advice so readily and for free: Marion Lindblad-Goldberg, Ph.D.; Beatrice Lazaroff, Ph.D.; and Barbara Noble, Ph.D.

Special thanks go to other professionals: Mark Nardone, editor of *Main Line Today* magazine, for his encouragement and candor; Vivian Lingard, my United Press International reporting cohort for her expertise in proofreading my book; Ken Bingham, my thesis adviser, for his guidance and for teaching me how to write a winning nonfiction book proposal; and authors R. Foster Winans, of Writers Room of Bucks County, and Michael Bamberger for their insightful advice.

I'd love to thank all my friends who have been so supportive of my efforts, but to list their names would mess with the pagination. So I'll mention by name only those who appear in the book. They are Francine Bank, who is forgiven for insisting I call that personal ad; Susie Zudick, who fixed me up; Fran Rosenbaum and Doris Grassi, my kindred spirits; Hilary Smith, whose enthusiasm kept me going; Jane and Joel Smith and Richard Simmons, who encouraged me to move on; Arnie Zudick, who hid his pleasure when my entering a relationship meant someone else would change my floodlights; and Jonathan Roth, who continued to date me even after learning about the book.

My family features prominently in this work because, let's face it, without them, there would be no story. So thanks first to my mom, Thelma, and my stepdad, Herb Sayare. You two set a standard for second marriages that is both admirable and heartening. And thanks to Dorothy Fisher, to whom mother-in-law jokes did not apply; to my sister, Susie Schultz, who patiently listened to the first draft of every chapter and begged for more; to my niece Neena and nephew Michael, who will now see a side of Aunt Ellie I've concealed for years.

And thanks to my daughter, Debra, who laid first eyes on every bit of copy that went into this book and whose admiration for me is surpassed only by my admiration for her. And to my son, Noah, who has kept me laughing and sane all these years and who probably won't read the book anyway.

Last, a thank-you goes to Charles Albert Fisher III. You raised the bar.

Index